Better Homes and Gardens®

DECORATING

IDEAS under $100

The contemporary calico print fabric on the far wall and partially revealed in the room divider sets the mood for a red, white, and blue color scheme in the living room that is pictured above. The warmth of the vibrant red is controlled nicely by an interplay of textures and patterns, wood floors with a natural finish, and broad expanses of neutral white background.

BETTER HOMES AND GARDENS BOOKS

Editorial Director: Don Dooley

Managing Editor: Malcolm E. Robinson   Art Director: John Berg

Asst. Managing Editor: Lawrence D. Clayton   Asst. Art Director: Randall Yontz

Senior Editor: Marie Schulz

Designers: Julie Zesch, Harijs Priekulis, Faith Berven

CONTENTS

Starting Out

All too often, advice on decorating involves basic color facts—monochromatic, analogous, and complementary color schemes; lighting information; furniture styles; furniture arrangement; and a host of other information that (sometimes) has the homemaker in a quandary. All she really wants is some sound advice on how to decorate her home for the least amount of money possible. Here is the problem-solving book that will provide answers to many of these questions—Decorating Ideas Under $100.

Each of the ideas illustrated in this book, or described in the easy-to-understand text, can be accomplished for less than $100; many for only a few dollars and a few hours of your leisure time. It may be just a suggestion that you take a piece of furniture that you already have in your home and revamp it—perhaps add a bright, new slipcover to a drab, upholstered chair or sofa, a fresh coat of paint or an interesting antique finish to a chest of drawers, or frames and mats for prints and family photos.

Those of you who have recently moved from one home or apartment to another may want to add one or more pieces of furniture, an area rug, new draperies, or an accessory or two. If this is the case, you will find many practical suggestions for adding to your furnishings with a minimum of expense.

And for those who plan to buy home furnishings items rather than to make them, or to hire skilled help for decorating, sewing, and carpentry projects, there are numerous tips that will help you receive the best value for the money you spend.

Instructions for making functional and decorative items for the home are included in every chapter. If you are a homemaker who is nimble-fingered and knowledgeable about the basic sewing techniques, and there is a handyman in the family who is willing to devote some of his leisure time to simple carpentry projects, the expenditures can be kept to the bare minimum.

Whether you choose to duplicate the ideas presented in this book, or to revise or adapt them to better fit your pattern of living is up to you. Then again, the ideas may encourage you to create something of your own that is completely original.

New products and improvements of existing products have resulted in an endless list of fabrics, paints, tiles, paneling, and carpeting in both natural and man-made materials. Production techniques, too, have improved a great deal within the last few years. Duplications of costly fabrics, metals, woods, and leathers are now priced well within the reach of the majority of consumers.

No longer do you have to be apprehensive about color choice of carpeting, draperies, or upholstery fabric because of the possibility of its fading; about fabrics that might shrink or show spots easily; or wood furniture whose finish becomes scarred or marred. Now, there are built-in qualities that add durability to the most fragile and elegant-appearing items in the home furnishings field.

These advances enable you to participate actively in the decorating and furnishing of your home, and to enjoy surroundings that are completely personal and geared to your way of life.

The contents of this book are geared to the questions homemakers most frequently ask about home decorating. Chapter heads were chosen with these questions in mind. Regardless of whether you are planning a complete decorating or redecorating project, updating a single room, or simply adding color or accent, there are many ideas that will be of interest to you. Both home owners and apartment dwellers are given consideration.

The basic principles of good design—choosing color combinations; developing an eye for good design, proper scale and balance—are interwoven throughout the text. There are many examples that point out how you can apply these principles.

As soon as you realize that decorating and furnishing a home in good taste does not necessarily involve the expenditure of a large sum of money, you are well on your way to accomplishing your decorating goals. The primary ingredients are enthusiasm, imagination, your talents and skills, and a few dollars. The satisfaction gained from contributing your own ideas, and your own handiwork to home decorating projects cannot be measured in dollars and cents. Moreover, good decorating contributes immensely to making family living a delightful experience.

Whether inexpensive or costly, old or new, or handmade or machine-made, accessories add the sparkle that changes an ordinary house into an inviting home. These are the family's personal items that add a note of individuality.

ACCESSORIES

Sugar 'n spice 'n everything nice — that's what accessories add to your home.

Accessories are usually classified as either decorative or functional. Decorative accessories are chosen for their beauty only — pictures on the wall (oil paintings, etchings, water colors, engravings, photographs); wall plaques; wall hangings; sculptured pieces; greenery and flowers; collectibles (lead soldiers, coins, shells, and rocks); and accent lighting. Functional accessories, on the other hand, have a practical as well as decorative value — a clock on the mantel; candlesticks; mirrors; bowls; vases; ash trays; pillows; and lamps.

There are other items that can be either functional or decorative. For example, a crystal pitcher is a functional accessory, while a crystal obelisk is a decorative accessory. This applies to many pewter, silver, copper, brass, ceramic, and porcelain accessories, too.

Accessories should be chosen to accent major furnishings. Not only will the right choice of accessories give character, warmth, and individuality to an otherwise bland and impersonal room, but it will also echo the preferences and interests of the family. On the following pages, you will find many suggestions for using accessories that you already have, and for buying and making accessories — all of them for less than $100.

First, consider the mood you wish to create in a room — formal or informal? You may achieve a formal mood by displaying your precious items in the living or dining room. Informal items, children's art, for example, can add a whimsical note to a breakfast room.

Second, consider the arrangement of accessories. While small accessories used singly seem unimportant, massed together they become interesting. A large accessory can be all by itself.

Keep in mind that objects related in spirit blend together well as long as size, scale, texture, and balance are considered, and they complement your decor.

Here's another aspect to consider when arranging accessories. When you place books on shelves, intersperse them with other accessories—a clock, a piece of pottery, a pewter mug, a figurine, a wood carving, or a brass bowl. You can use objects of all sizes, shapes, and materials, or a collection of related items.

Change accessories with the seasons. A grouping that gives a warm and comfortable feeling during the cold winter months may give way to more casual items during the summer.

If you go all-out when decorating your home for the Christmas season, take away some of the year-round accessories during this holiday period to avoid having a cluttered look.

Many accessories can be used year-round. A ceramic bowl that holds shiny red apples in the fall can be used for oranges and nuts at Christmas time. The same bowl can be heaped with decorated eggs at Easter time, and later on it can be used to display garden flowers.

USING WHAT YOU HAVE ALREADY

Take a look at what you already have before you buy any accessories. Make a careful search and you may unearth interesting items you had completely forgotten about. Often, there are items right in your home that can take their place as handsome accessories. Some can be used just as they are; others may need restoring. For example, old family photos, resurrected from the bottom of a drawer, may be matted and framed and displayed in a family room or den.

Part of the joy of collecting is sharing your interest with others, so get out your collections—coins, soldiers, keys, cups and saucers, to name just a few—and display them in decorative groupings that will enhance your furnishings.

Hand-me-downs from relatives and friends are another good source of accessories. An old sugar bowl might hold a small green plant; a hand-painted tray may fit into a wall grouping.

Notice the careful attention given to proportion, scale, and arrangement in groupings of eclectic accessories in the room below. Prints, paintings, glass, crystal, brass, books, pillows, greenery, and flowers have been combined to add decorative interest to a room with a neutral background.

Create a wall of family photos. Fasten wood or aluminum T molding to wall, spaced so 8 x 10-inch prints mounted on illustration board will slip between. Get 8 x 10 prints made from negatives. Have prints dry mounted, or use adhesive. Price, not including cost of prints, about $24.

Family photos have entered the accessory picture (no pun intended). For years they were kept out of sight and subject only to infrequent viewing; now, they play an important role in decorating. Regardless of whether they are portraits taken by a professional photographer or candid shots taken by a camera enthusiast, they can take their place as decorative accessories, along with others that you have around the house.

If you have old family photos that are already framed and matted, use them as they are. If the frames are shabby, give them a good cleaning first. If this doesn't restore the frames to their original appearance, refinish them in a wood-tone or metallic finish. Part of the beauty of old family photos lies in the fact that they are usually a variety of sizes and shapes. The combination of oval, round, square, and rectangular shapes offers many wall grouping possibilities.

Newer family photos can be included in a wall grouping with the old family pictures, or they can constitute a grouping of their own. Wedding and graduation photos, and pictures of children and families fall in this category.

Snapshots, either in black and white or in color, can be used in their original size or enlarged. If you use them in their original size, you can frame them singly in mini-frames or buy long, slender frames that hold two, three, or even more small pictures. Also available are large, partitioned frames that hold from 12 to 20 small photos which can be inserted or removed.

Enlarged snapshots of athletic events, holiday get-togethers, and historic and scenic vacation spots can be matted and framed to form an accessory grouping that is loaded with action. Inexpensive stock frames of narrow black molding cost from 59¢ to $2, depending on the size of the picture being framed. These are fine for displaying your glossy prints. You can buy mat board at an art supply store and cut it to size. The mat width should be ½ to 1 inch wider at the bottom than it is at the top or sides of the picture. For example, if you are placing a 6 x 8-inch picture in a 9 x 12-inch frame, cut the mat so that it is 2½ inches wide at the bottom and 1½ inches wide at the top and the sides. Mat board is available in a wide range of colors.

Collecting is fun, and it is something that everyone in the family can enjoy. When collectibles are used in the home, the search becomes even more satisfying. Collections can be used to good advantage as decorative accessories as long as they are grouped and displayed in an interesting manner, and in the appropriate setting.

A collection of delicate demitasse cups and saucers is ideal in a dining room with traditional furnishings, whereas pewter, copper, brass, or earthenware objects are more compatible with country-style or provincial furnishings. Athletic trophies, pop art posters, and record jackets from albums of favorite recording artists might be the collections teen-agers would choose to display in their rooms. A boating enthusiast might collect signal flags to add interest to a family room with a nautical theme. A collection of car license plates mounted on the walls of the garage or workshop might help to create the right atmosphere for the amateur mechanic.

Hand-me-downs from family and friends can provide great no-cost accessories if you use your imagination and ingenuity. In addition to their decorative value, they often bring back memories of happy childhood days and the people who were close to you. They have an intrinsic value regardless of whether they are precious antiques or merely outmoded items.

Even if your kitchen is completely modern and outfitted with efficient appliances, it might be a more pleasant work area if you inject a note from the past—a collection of old wooden spoons hanging on the wall, or a row of green glass fruit jars in pint, quart, and two-quart sizes on the counter rather than the usual canister set. Bowls and relish dishes of cut glass that can hold candy, fruit, or flowers lend themselves well to either traditional or contemporary room settings. Crocks, butter churns, and coffee grinders are natural accents for rooms with wood-paneled walls and country-style furnishings.

Both collectibles and hand-me-downs are used imaginatively as accessories in this bachelor apartment. Everything from original art to posters, Mexican pottery, and colorful pillows are displayed in an eye-catching manner. The bird cage on the wall gives the entire arrangement depth and added interest.

A collection of old keys hanging from small hooks adds interest to the solid-color vinyl-covered walls in a child's room. A large key was attached to each tieback that holds the draperies in place. This type of arrangement allows plenty of space for adding to the collection in the future.

Inexpensive, stock-sized frames were used as a setting for the collection of seashells above. Velveteen was used for the background, and each shell glued onto it. The same treatment could be used for other collectibles—pine cones, coasters, stones, Indian arrowheads, or any small items that interest you.

Lots of little items, both old and new, form an exciting arrangement in a kitchen corner. The wall-hung cabinet with dividers provides display area for a collection of antique egg cups and other small objects. The ventilating fan above the range is a part of the arrangement of pop art and primitive masks.

A collection of Americana, handed down in the family, is in character with antique furnishings and rough-hewn stone walls of the family room below. Earthenware jugs, bowls, and pitchers in warm, mellow tones are accented with green plants to form a striking background for the rugged, old Franklin stove. A large jug was converted into the table lamp.

12

ADDING ACCESSORIES

Have you recently redecorated a room, or added one or more pieces of beautiful new furniture, yet found yourself slightly disappointed because the room still didn't have quite the sparkle that you had anticipated? Before you despair completely, try adding some accessories. They are considered by many experts to be the key to successful decorating. Perhaps a brightly colored pillow, brass candlesticks, a wicker basket, a crystal decanter, a mirrored tray, or even a bulletin board will add that all-important touch of individuality that the room still lacks.

You may already have pillows on the sofa, but perhaps one or two made of fur, or fake fur will add textural interest. You can even combine the long-haired, fluffy-type with the striped or spotted jungle-look pillows. If yours is a traditional or country decorating theme, you might choose crewelwork or needlepoint pillows. You can purchase these pillows ready-made, or you can buy a kit in a needlework department and make them yourself.

Often, a change in arrangement is all you need to add interest to a room. For example, if you have a pair of candlesticks placed on either side of a bowl or vase on a table or buffet, break away from this traditional arrangement. Get out all the candleholders you have—short ones, tall ones, metal, glass, ceramic. Then, buy an assortment of candles of different sizes, shapes, and in a variety of colors that are harmonious with furnishings in the room. Place the candles in holders and arrange them together in a grouping of different colors and varying heights.

A child's room that features a circus theme may need just a little more color. If so, hang a cluster of brightly colored balloons in a corner, close to the ceiling where they are out of reach of inquisitive little fingers. Use both round and oval balloons in several sizes.

If you have a Boy Scout in the family who is the troop bugler, show him how proud you are of his musical accomplishments by keeping the bugle brightly polished and by hanging it on the wall of his room where it can be admired.

An antique umbrella stand, an accessory that is both useful and decorative, was purchased in a thrift shop. It was painted stark white to contrast with charcoal-colored walls and floor in the entryway above. The charcoal and white treatment was chosen to pick up the same colors as those in the cabinet in the foreground. There are numerous antiques, such as this, that are available in a wide range of prices.

There are still many apartments and homes that have an old-fashioned radiator such as the one in the picture at the left. Why not take advantage of its decorating possibilities rather than try to de-emphasize or ignore it—it won't disappear anyway. Here, the radiator was treated to a coat of black enamel and topped with a stained plywood slab. Add a few accessories, and you have a real conversation piece.

If you feel that you need one more spot of color in a room, why not change your present telephone for one of a different color? For a truly elegant look, you can even replace your phone with an ornate, decorator cradle-type telephone trimmed with graceful gold scroll decorations.

Tall vases and pitchers are other good accessory items. Don't tuck them away when the blooming season is over; use them year-round. Whatever you do, make the most of the familiar natural things that surround you. For example, if you live in a cotton-growing area, take a few stalks that have fluffy white cotton bolls, and display them in a tall container. Or if you live in the grain belt, bring the fields into your home by showing off a sheaf of wheat in a brass or earthenware vase. If you want an exotic arrangement, buy a few peacock feathers or gather up cattails, dried grasses, and silver shillings and arrange them in a tall container.

Many people have a lovely cut-glass decanter on a table, buffet, or shelf. If you have one of these, make the most of it by placing the decanter on a tray and surrounding it with cordial glasses. The grouping will be more decorative than was the single, lonely item, and it will be useful when you serve guests, too.

If you have a ceramic, wooden, or metal bowl resting on a table or buffet, fill it with fruit. Red or golden yellow apples, bunches of grapes, and oranges make a colorful arrangement.

On a dressing tabletop that tends to get cluttered, add a mirrored or enameled tray to hold the collection of jars and perfume bottles in an attractive and colorful arrangement. This will also protect wood surfaces from spillage.

Even a bay window, the envy of most homemakers, may need something added in the way of accessories. Try hanging baskets of delicate, lacelike ferns in the bay, and this area may turn out to be the focal point of the entire room.

In a den, family room, or breakfast room, hang a large bulletin board covered with brightly colored fabric, felt, or burlap. Use it to post coming events—TV programs, movie and theater offerings, and athletic event schedules. Revise the listing frequently to keep it up-to-date.

Transforming the bleak bathroom above into the colorful one at the right cost less than $100. The striped awning, made from a shower curtain and held in place with suspension-type rods, started the yellow, orange, turquoise, and avocado color scheme. Yellow enameled bamboo orange trees, and freestanding shelves are made of spindles connected by threaded dowels. Shelves of ¾-inch plywood have ¾-inch holes drilled at corners to accommodate dowel connectors. Branches are bent wire coat hangers covered with green vinyl tape. Leaves are made of two layers of velvet adhesive-backed paper. Oranges, hung with paper clips, are styrofoam balls covered with papier mâché and spray-painted. Colors are repeated in flowers and leaves embroidered on a $7.95 turquoise rug and lid cover set, and in guest soap in a ceramic compote on the counter. Flowers on shelf were a craft project, and tissue holder below is a covered shoe box.

BUYING ACCESSORIES UNDER $100

After you have arranged all the accessories you already had, and those you have acquired from your family and friends, take a close look at each room. See if you still need one or more objects to complete your decorating project to your satisfaction. If you feel that more accessories are necessary for your purpose, give it some careful thought, and don't rush out and buy the first thing you see that appeals to you. Acquiring accessories is something that does not have to be done in a big hurry. It's much more fun to purchase one item at a time.

Start by doing a little research. Browse through gift shops, decorator shops, model rooms and homes, museum shops, and art galleries. Also, look through home decorating magazines and books for suggestions on just what accessories to buy and how to use them tastefully. Spending some time at thrift shops, art fairs, and auctions might help, too.

Return to these places when you decide just what you want, and chances are you'll find what you are looking for. Whether you are looking for a handcrafted Mexican mask or merely a soap dish for the powder room, shopping for accessories can be exciting. Keep in mind that you will probably have to live with whatever you buy for a long time, so be sure it pleases you. Although a certain piece may be the right price, nothing is a bargain unless you genuinely like it.

Functional accessories are those that perform a practical service and are decorative as well. If your decorating budget is limited, you should consider buying this type of item first.

Perhaps you feel that a mirror for the entryway is the most important item at present. If so, consider the size and shape of the room, and the mood of the decorating scheme. Which would be most appropriate, a round, oval, square, or rectangular mirror? Even a small entryway can hold quite a large mirror because it will visually double the size of the hall. Also, there are usually only a few pieces of furniture in an entryway—a small table or shelf, a chair, or a bench. If you have a formal and elegant theme, select a mirror with an ornate gold frame. If you have country-style furnishings, choose one with a wood frame in walnut or maple finish. In a hall that features contemporary design, your choice could be a mirror with a sliver of shiny metal frame or with no frame at all.

The price of a mirror depends on its size, the quality of mirror glass used, and the type of frame used for the mirror. Top-quality mirrors are made of twin-ground, polished ¼-inch plate glass. Those with frames may have a beveled edge; those without frames, seamed or polished edge. Most inexpensive mirrors are made of sheet or window glass, which is not polished or ground. Because of this, they may not present a perfect reflection. Thickness determines the quality of window glass used for mirrors.

A captivating wall decoration that portrays a family of contemporary owls is an exact reproduction of a unique, welded metal sculpture. It is available in a gold metal or walnut finish. Price is about $25.

Sunburst wall clock and four chessmen, which are copies of hand-carved originals, come in either metallic gold or silver finish. The battery-operated clock retails for about $30; the chessmen, about $4 each.

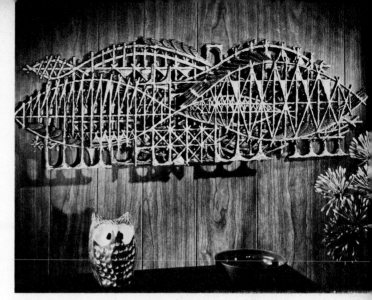

Rare coin plaques, faithfully reproduced and finished in gleaming metal gold, surround an American crest plaque in traditional colors. Large plaque sells for about $18; the set of four coin plaques, about $13.

This impressionistic wall panorama, finished in gleaming metal gold with flashes of color, measures 35 x 11 inches. Reproduced in deep-dimensional detail from a handcrafted original, it sells for about $40.

A clock is another important item that falls in the functional accessory category. The price range is wide, and there are clocks designed for every room in the home. They range in size from tiny jewelled clocks intended to rest on a bedside table in a very feminine boudoir that you can buy for around $10 all the way to tall, grandfather clocks that may cost several hundred dollars. There are brightly colored clocks for children's rooms that have large numbers instead of the usual Roman numerals; these aid small tots in learning to tell time. Best of all, they are inexpensive to buy.

No matter what style of furnishings you have, you can find a clock in a size and design that blends with your decorating scheme—and that fits within your budget. There are electric, cordless, digital, and key-wound clocks. A silent version may be just right for bedrooms where silence is golden, but a tick-tock in the living room extends a welcome to all who enter.

Candleholders, vases, ash trays, lamps, fireplace equipment, bookends, and desk appointments are all examples of functional accessories. Most of these are inexpensive items that you should purchase before buying decorative accessories. It doesn't matter whether you are shopping for a pair of bookends to hold a few of your very special volumes, or an ash tray to rest on a table, give each purchase the consideration you would when buying major furnishings.

Decorative accessories are chosen simply to add beauty and character to their surroundings. They are the completely personal items that express family interests and tastes, and the list is almost endless. There are pictures; plaques; sculptured pieces; greenery; collectibles; figurines; metal, crystal, and porcelain objects; and accent lighting. Prices can range from 65¢ for a wood trivet from India to an exorbitant figure for a highly prized jade collection.

You always hear tales about a friend of a friend who found a true Sevres vase in a second-hand store and paid practically nothing for it, or someone else who put in a high bid of $5 at an auction and wound up with a badly tarnished silver coffeepot that turned out to be one made by Joseph Anthony, Jr. in the year 1800. These finds are few and far between. Usually, it takes a lot of time and perseverance to locate valuable antiques and, except in very rare cases, they are expensive. So, be realistic and buy accessories that are in tune with your budget.

For example, you might experience difficulty in finding an oil painting for less than $100 that you like, but you can find many other types of beautiful and well-designed wall hangings that are inexpensive. There are lovely water colors; limited edition etchings, engravings, and lithographs; and fabric wall hangings. For a room with a contemporary theme, there are large serigraphs, carpet, or plexiglass wall hangings.

This highly individual-looking wall tapestry that adds depth to a tiny study area is really a rug. In shades of browns, russets, and gold, it adds textural interest and complements furniture and accessories. This rug sells for about $100, but there are rugs in all prices and sizes from which to choose.

Impressive bookends in the form of fierce Spanish Conquistadors look and feel like heavy cast bronze sculpture. Each one measures 7⅞ inches tall, 4 inches wide, and 2⅞ inches thick. A handsome accent for Mediterranean furnishings in any room, the pair is priced under $25 in giftware departments.

Finding these inexpensive accessories is not nearly as difficult as you might imagine. Almost every community boasts of at least one import shop where you can buy a variety of artifacts from foreign countries. An African carving or a Peruvian mask might be perfect in your den or family room. A ceramic jug or vase from Mexico, with its handcrafted look, may be just the right container to hold an arrangement of dried materials. Oriental wind chimes are an interesting accessory for a patio or a breakfast room. A chunky object of Scandinavian crystal will add sparkle to a room that seems subdued.

When you are buying accessories, don't forget the man of the house. If he is the type who reads the stock quotations each morning before he indulges in breakfast conversation, why not pamper him? Show that you share his enthusiasm for the world of finance by getting him a miniature version of a charging bull in a shiny or oxidized metal for his desk. If he is engaged in international trade, buy him a world globe. If his hobby is coin collecting, have one or more coins encased in a plexiglass paperweight. If he yearns for a life at sea, place a replica of a clipper ship on the fireplace mantel. None of these personal items that mean so much to their owner need cost a great deal of money.

Bedroom accessories are very good examples of accessories that can range in price from a few cents to many dollars. They run the gamut from a conservative wicker basket that holds sewing and knitting materials to delicately cut crystal perfume bottles. It is best to concentrate your spending on the most necessary items first. For the sake of comfort and convenience, the bed-side table should have a lamp with an easy-to-reach switch, a clock, and some space for a few books or magazines. This is also a good place for an extension telephone.

A folding luggage rack takes a minimum of storage space and is invaluable for someone who packs and unpacks frequently, and for guests. A valet rack is a big help to the man of the house when every minute counts.

When you choose items for your own pleasure and convenience, start with a pot of African violets if you must watch the budget. You can always add a silver-backed hand mirror, a vacuum pitcher that keeps beverages either hot or cold, a jewelry chest, or a music box later.

Closet accessories that keep wearing apparel and household items well organized need not tax your budget, either. These accessories make it possible for you to open closet doors with complete disregard, perhaps even with pride.

Also available are matched accessories—garment bags, shoe bags, hat boxes, storage boxes. They are color-coordinated in solid, patterned, striped, or see-through vinyl fabric. Special storage bags protect fur garments, which should never be encased in vinyl because it is airtight. There are closet organizers that you can arrange to make the best use of every inch of space. Racks that fit on the backs of closet doors hold shoes and purses. There are even hangers for coats, suits, skirts, and trousers; and padded hangers that protect the shoulder line of garments. These cost no more than a few dollars.

Kitchen accessories no longer are limited to purely functional items such as a canister set or a cookie jar, and most of them cost no more than just a few dollars. Make room to grow a pot of herbs, or display a few shiny copper or brass, or handcrafted pottery objects. Colorful cookware designed to travel from oven to table is worthy of display between meals, also.

Be sure to hang accessories on kitchen walls. If wall space is limited, you may have to settle for a clock and a few pieces of children's art. If you have an expansive wall, hang a few pictures, a cross-stitch sampler, a wall sconce, and a spice or spoon rack. For about $25 you can buy enough for a wall grouping.

Bathroom accessories can completely alter the character of a humdrum, purely functional area. You don't have to stick to the decorating style and colors that prevail in the rest of the rooms. Even if you have antiques or traditional furnishings in your home, you can switch to something completely different in the bathroom.

Perhaps you've grown weary of your pastel blue bathroom with its yellow towels, rug, and shower curtain. In all probability, the blue fixtures, tile, and floor are there to stay, but you can give the bathroom an inexpensive face lifting with new accessories. Buy a purple rug; purple, blue, and dark green towels; and a dark green shower curtain. Fill a small purple bowl with blue guest soap, place a pot of violets on the counter, hang a wall hanging that repeats the same colors, and add a crystal tumbler and perfume bottles for sparkle.

Shower curtains, towel sets, rugs and carpeting, and bath mats come in many colors and patterns. Clothes hampers; tissue dispensers; soap dishes; and towel racks, rings, poles, and trees are available in many materials. For a formal atmosphere, choose gold or silver filigree; for a contemporary feeling, you can pick from clear lucite, plexiglass, and lacquered or metal finishes; and for a country theme, use wood tones.

The once-familiar trade symbols of the pharmacist, pawnbroker, harnessmaker, and bootmaker have been faithfully reproduced in wall plaques that measure 12 x 9 inches. They can be grouped together, or they can be scattered among a collection of pictures and other wall hangings. They retail for about $7.

This giant-sized wall sconce of Mediterranean design has a background of intertwining acanthus leaves and three sweeping arms that hold candles aloft. It measures 11¾ x 36½ inches high, and comes in either a pecan wood tone or polychrome finish. The price for the sconce and gold candles is about $60.

This wall hanging in a child's room is a group of posters glued to a piece of tempered hardboard, edged with molding strips, and painted a bright color. To protect posters, apply a coat of clear varnish. When dry, frame posters with black electrician's tape.

A collection of paintings, prints, and three-dimensional objects gives interest to a room devoid of color. The horizontal pastel of Mexican children has subtle coloring; the floral oil beneath has intense colors. The enamel above balloon print adds balance.

MAKING ACCESSORIES

Not everyone has as much talent as Picasso and Michelangelo in wielding a paint brush and palette. Nor does everyone have the skill to chisel a piece of stone or marble into an object of grace and beauty. But anyone who has some imagination and can follow simple instructions can create something for the home that is both decorative and relatively inexpensive.

Making accessories will often fall into the category of a hobby—ceramics, weaving, metalwork, drawing, or painting. If you want to explore a hobby that requires professional instruction, there are adult education classes at schools and art centers that offer courses.

However, there are other accessories that you can learn to make simply by following step-by-step instructions found in various magazines and books. For example, you can make a very attractive vase from an empty wine bottle that has an interesting shape. Simply glue a number of small stones and shells of various colors and shapes in a random arrangement.

You may think it impossible to create a piece of sculpture with no investment, but this is not true. To start with, turn a wire frame of coat hangers into a sculptured shape. Then, tear old newspapers into narrow strips and immerse a few at a time in flour and water paste. Wrap strips around the wire frame, a layer at a time, and shape it into the form you desire. Don't do many layers at one time, or it will be difficult for the paste to dry. After the entire sculpture is completed, spray it with white, black, or metallic paint, and no one but you will know that underneath it all beats a heart of papier mâché.

Assembling model ships, cars, airplanes, and trains is a hobby that can be shared by father and son, and the finished models can be proudly displayed on bookshelves, desks, tables, or any other place where they will stand out.

How to mat, frame, and arrange pictures is a topic that appeals to many home decorators. You don't have to be an artist, and you don't have to have a machine shop in the basement to accomplish satisfying results with a minimum of expense, time, and labor.

Unless you are framing an oil painting, be sure to get a frame with glass. Frames with glareproof glass cost a little more than those with regular glass, but they are desirable if pictures will hang where they reflect the light from the sun, or a lamp or lighting fixture.

Making your own frames is not difficult, and it doesn't take a lot of tools, but a miter box corner clamp will make the task easier. You can buy moldings to create any design of frame you choose. Cut the frame pieces on a 45-degree angle so that the corners will be perfectly mitered. Put a rabbet (a groove into which the picture will fit) in the back of the frame. If you are framing an oil painting, tack the canvas to a wood molding and fit it into the rabbet. If you are framing a picture that will be matted and covered with glass, the depth of the rabbet must be adjusted to accommodate all three thicknesses. Glue the frame sections together and clamp them together until the glue is dry.

Frames can be finished with paint, metallic finishes, or stains and varnish. For a distressed finish, tap completed frame lightly with a hammer or sharp object and sand lightly to remove splinters before applying the finish.

Mat board is available in many colors at art supply shops. Use a sharp mat knife to cut the board, and be sure to have a wider border at the bottom edge than at the sides or at the top.

A very large picture can hang over a mantel or sofa and be the center of interest in a room. Smaller pictures should be grouped on one wall rather than hung individually. Combine pictures of various sizes and shapes. Don't group them too close together but close enough to present a unified appearance. Allow space for adding pictures. In an entryway where they will be viewed from a standing position, hang pictures at eye level of an average person's height. In rooms where they will be viewed from a sitting position, they should be hung lower.

A contemporary thread construction is inexpensive and easy to make. Contrasting threads and background color will make it an exciting wall hanging for your home. You will need ½-inch plywood about 18 x 24 inches, a ¼-inch batten strip about 8 feet long, a 1 x 3 two feet long, epoxy, crochet thread, ¾-inch brads, and one jar of flat water paint.

Cut plywood to 18 x 24-inch size; cut two batten strips 24 inches long, and two 18½ inches long. Glue and nail strips to edge of plywood to form frame. Sand surface. Cut 1 x 3 in half and then crosswise to form four wedges. Arrange three of them in a triangle design as shown, alternating high and low ends of wedges. Draw guidelines with a straightedge to mark placement of wedges. Glue wedges to plywood.

Draw a line down the middle of each wedge top, marking off at ½-inch intervals. Nail a brad at every interval, letting about ⅛ inch protrude. Pound same number of nails in each wedge. Paint entire construction, nails and all. Two coats may be necessary in order to cover completely.

When paint is dry, attach the crochet thread. Knot the first end to the lowest brad and wind it around the lowest brad on the next wedge. Continue to the last wedge, and then bring it back to the first one, and wind around the next lowest brad. Continue winding in this manner until each brad has a thread around it; then knot and cut at final brad.

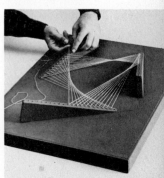

In the room above an entire wall is decorated with less fabric than it takes to make the average dress. To create this gigantic wall hanging that is easy, quick, and inexpensive, simply stretch two yards of colorful fabric with large motifs over a frame of 1 x 2s and tack it securely. It weighs so little that it can be hung with stick-on picture hooks.

Wall hangings that you create yourself are often as spectacular as a costly oil painting or tapestry. The material that you use can be as inexpensive or as costly as your budget permits. Whether or not the hangings are an effective decorative accent depends more on your choice of color, pattern, texture, size, and shape than it does on the price of the material used.

One of the quickest and easiest ways to make a wall hanging is to use fabric. There are cottons, linens, wools, silks, synthetics, and blends in drapery, upholstery, and dress goods fabrics that are suitable for wall hangings. If you can find a discontinued sample, or a remnant with the colors and pattern that will highlight your furnishings, the cost will be very little. Even if the pattern of your choice is on a brand new bolt, the price for one or two yards is a small investment to obtain the color and interest a wall hanging adds to a room.

When you shop for fabric for a wall hanging, keep in mind the color scheme, the character, and the size of the room in which it will hang. If you have a large expanse of white wall, you may want to cover a large area. If you hang it vertically, from floor to ceiling, it will add height to the room. If it runs horizontally, the room will appear longer and lower. In an entryway, or over a desk, one yard of fabric may be just right. In a bedroom, you might choose a panel as wide as the bed that stretches from floor to ceiling behind the headboard. It could even continue up onto the ceiling.

There are several different ways to hang fabric wall hangings. You can simply insert the fabric in a frame and hang it as you would a picture, or you can stretch it on a wood frame. If you choose to do the latter, make the frame of 2 x 2s so the finished hanging will be light enough to hang as you would a picture. All you

If your budget won't stretch to include an original painting, compromise with a large print from a museum, book, or art supply store. Glue it to a piece of hardboard and frame with a wallpaper border, mitering at corners. Spray with plastic finish. Cost: $17.

Construct this candelabrum frame from ½-inch square aluminum bar stock. Cut pieces with a hacksaw, fastening joints with self-tapping metal screws put in from the back. Use epoxy resin cement to glue on coasters to hold votive candles in glass containers. Spray with flat black paint, and hang with metal angle brackets.

In a teen-age girl's bedroom, you can make a wall hanging similar to the one above at very little cost. Use hardboard for the back. A mirror, mounted in the center, is surrounded by greeting cards. Use black vinyl tape to form separations, and frame with picture molding painted black.

Create your own conversation piece "painting" with two widths of a large scale, brilliantly patterned wallpaper. Paste wallpaper to a sheet of 48 x 52-inch hardboard. Frame picture with batten strips nailed or glued to the edges of the picture. Then, spray with plastic spray for dust protection. One single roll of wallpaper is all that is required.

The dramatic wall hanging below, that could pass for an expensive tapestry, is easy and inexpensive to make. It is simply a beach towel mounted on cafe curtain rods. All you have to do is fold over a 1½-inch hem at each end to form a channel for the rods. You can either sew the hem, glue it down with fabric glue, or use double-faced pressure-sensitive tape.

have to do is make a hem at the top and the bottom wide enough to insert the rods.

One of the easiest ways to hang fabric wall hangings is to use double-faced pressure-sensitive tape. Turn under the rough edges and selvage of the fabric, and hem. Lay the fabric flat with the wrong side facing up, and apply tape to all four sides, about ¼ inch from edge. When you place the fabric on the wall, fasten the top edge first. Pull away about 12 inches of the paper backing strip from the tape, and press that part of the fabric to the wall, applying enough pressure to make it adhere securely. Continue to pull off backing and press fabric in place. When the top edge is secure, pull off the backing on side edges and press the sides in place, pulling the fabric taut to eliminate air pockets. Secure bottom edge last.

Wallpaper can be used for highly original, inexpensive wall hangings equally as well as fabric, and the choice of colors, patterns, and textures is just as varied. In the traditional set-ting, select a wallpaper with the appearance of tapestry or a very elegant and formal flocked pattern. In a contemporary setting, select a shiny metallic, or a glistening, wet-look vinyl-coated wallpaper. Whatever your choice of wallpaper, hang it as you would a fabric wall hanging, or use wallpaper paste. Always follow manufacturer's directions printed on the back.

Wall hangings of carpeting, or small area rugs, may be of a solid color, a geometric design, or an oriental rug pattern. In addition to color and pattern, carpeting adds textural interest. These wall hangings can be framed, mounted on hardboard, or fastened directly to the wall.

Mount felt or burlap in solid colors on hardboard, used as is, or trimmed in many different ways. In a den, or family room, add an unusual design by pinning on losing tickets from the racetrack. In a feminine bedroom, decorate with old-fashioned sentimental Valentines or greeting cards. For a sewing or hobby room, make a collage of braid, yarn, a thimble, a

Here's a masculine touch that you can add to a boy's room, or to a family room or den. These large maps, used as wall hangings, are colorful and highly detailed navigational charts of ocean and coastal waterways. You can obtain them from the Coast Guard for only $1 each. Mount them on heavy illustration board with spray adhesive, then make the frames from walnut strips. Rabbet the back edges of the frames to receive the mounted charts and make half lap joints at the corners. You should be able to make two of these large map wall hangings for about $8. Finish with a coat of clear acrylic spray.

You don't even have to know which end of a needle to thread to accomplish some pretty spectacular things with fabrics these days. The wall hanging below is a good example. It is simply a panel of cotton drapery fabric in a bold design, mounted on a lightweight wood frame. Make the frame from 2 x 2s, and paint it to match the background color in the fabric. Fabric and frame weigh so little that the oversized hanging can be mounted on the wall with ordinary picture hooks. The bold pattern and sharp color contrast of the fabric wall hanging brighten up the neutral tones of a wood-paneled wall.

The wall hanging above is made from a travel poster that has been matted in white and placed in a narrow black frame. A coat of lacquer was added for dust protection. Against the black and white wall, it presents a pleasing contrast in color and design.

In the photo above a small area rug that resembles a Mondrian painting is the focal point of a room with stark white walls. The furniture, accessories, and the rug on the floor carry out the same vivid and dramatic colors as those in the rug wall hanging.

zipper, and a pair of scissors on a brightly colored felt background. Whatever your interests, try to incorporate one or more of them into a theme for a wall hanging that is completely individual.

There are primitives-on-wood available in kit form that will lend distinction to any room in your home. Sets that contain two or three primitives range from $11 to $30, depending on size. Each kit contains wood, paint, brushes, and detailed instructions for making these colorful paintings that have a "collector's look."

If you're eager to acquire some modern art wall hangings, but are dubious about your own creative talents, you can buy kits to make modern abstracts. One of these wall hangings is sure to be a conversation piece in any contemporary or eclectic room setting. All the materials for two abstracts, plus a scanner that shows you just how to translate your original design to a specially-treated board, and the wood for framing can be purchased for about $11 to $15 in hobby shops.

There is another type of do-it-yourself art that, in Europe, is referred to as Poppy Art. It is based on the punch-out, pop-up principle. There are square or circular designs constructed of white, heavyweight, plastic-coated paper, die-cut so that sections can be folded back to expose a contrasting color. One, two, or many sections can be folded back. It just depends on what mood you want to create. These unusual art objects come framed and ready to hang; the contrasting colors underneath that show through the die-cuts are silver or red. They retail for about $20 each.

Plexiglass makes a good background for contemporary wall hangings, too. Buy a square or rectangular piece, in either the clear or smoky gray tint, and glue on designs cut from carpet samples. Be sure to have your designs arranged before you start gluing.

For casual fall entertaining, fold a straw place mat around a sheaf of wheat and secure with rug yarn. Place wheat and a small houseplant to the rear of a wooden salad bowl. Make flowers of moistened corn husks, bent into petal shapes, and secured with wire.

For this composition of plum blooms, place needlepoint in bowl, cut branches of varying lengths, and secure them in a loose fan in bowl. Select one extralong branch and carefully bend it with your thumbs into an oval shape. Insert it behind plum blooms.

When your garden flowers are almost gone and you need a high back-of-the-table arrangement for an informal dinner party, combine a variety of berried branches with sprays of highbush cranberry into a graceful composition in your favorite brass container.

Floral arrangements add beauty to the home and impart a spirit of hospitality and gracious living. Whether you have a flower garden of your own or simply buy your flowers at a florist shop or greenhouse, you can enjoy flower arranging without spending a great deal of money.

During the growing season, when flowers are plentiful and inexpensive, you can use them lavishly. When they are scarce and costly, you can still have inexpensive arrangements if you combine just a few flowers with plant materials, rocks, shells, and weathered wood. A rose in a bud vase, a stem of iris mingled with iris foliage and a few seed pods, or one peony surrounded by its own leaves can all be appealing accents.

With flower arranging, just as in all creative areas, some people have a flair for it, while others have to study and practice to develop a degree of skill. For those who are eager to learn, there are flower arranging classes sponsored by garden clubs and adult education programs. Florists, too, share expert advice with amateurs; there are also many books and magazines featuring detailed instructions on this art.

You can create a tall, striking floral arrangement by combining brightly colored tulips with branches of varying lengths in a ceramic compote. Be sure to keep the size of the arrangement in proportion to the size of the table on which it will be displayed.

Every room in the home deserves to have some flowers. Here, bachelor buttons and daisy mums are combined and arranged in a pottery container that picks up the color scheme. The arrangement is in scale with the size of the table and height of the lamp.

Flower arranging is a fascinating hobby and it takes very little equipment. All you really need—other than flowers and foliage—are: several containers in basic shapes; an assortment of needlepoint holders and other stem-securing devices; a sharp knife or flower shears; and some florist's tape and clay.

There are no hard and fast rules in flower arranging, but there are principles of good design. If you use a tall vase, the height of flower materials should extend above the rim 1½ to 2 times the height of the vase. In shallow containers, the tallest stem should be 1½ to 2 times the length or diameter of the bowl. Balance may be symmetrical—two halves identical or nearly identical—or asymmetrical—halves are not equal but appear to have equal weight or importance.

A thing of beauty is a joy forever—nowhere are these words of wisdom more evident than in the choice of accessories for the home. Whether you are buying or making accessories, or have fallen heir to family treasures, treat them with the consideration they deserve.

On a long, low coffee table such as the one below, you can use a large mass of flowers arranged in a shallow container. It will add beauty to the furniture grouping and, because it is a very low arrangement, will not interfere with conversation among guests.

There are creative guidelines for wall and door treatments that set the stage for your furnishings. You can decorate walls and doors with a wide range of materials to achieve a subtle background or a bold focus, to visually alter the dimensions of a room, or to conceal awkward architectural features.

WALLS & DOORS

Today, there are many ways to decorate the walls and doors of a room for less than $100. You are no longer limited to a fresh coat of paint selected from an assortment of ready-mixed, bland colors. Decorating can be as dynamic and imaginative as you wish. This is made possible by the many new materials that are now available and by the refinement of the old, familiar products.

There are a host of wall coverings to choose from: paint, wallpaper, fabric, tile, paneling, leatherlike fabrics, vinyl-coated materials, cork, murals, stone, brick, or even shingles.

Although many of the interesting new materials are relatively inexpensive, paint is still the least expensive wall treatment available. With the custom-mixing service that most paint dealers offer, color selection is almost unlimited. However, even the most costly material, if used on one wall only, can create a beautiful background and still fit within the confines of a limited budget.

Wall treatments, in addition to giving a unique touch to a room, are architecturally important, too. You can camouflage defects, create visual impressions, and achieve remarkable results with unbending walls. With the correct choice of material, you can highlight features such as a fireplace, a bay window, or built-in bookshelves.

Similar decorating effects can be produced with doors, too. Today, doors are an important feature that should harmonize with the style and color scheme of a room's furnishings. You can use doors to enhance the decor by adding moldings and sculptured motifs, by covering them with fabric, vinyl, or grillwork panels, or by painting them.

Whatever type of material you choose, you can use it to transform your walls and doors into a colorful and dramatic background. They will work wonders for the appearance of your room, and the furnishings you have will take on new importance.

PAINT AND WALLPAPER

The four walls comprise the largest area of a room's background. What you do to these walls determines whether they will be the focal point of a room, or simply a backdrop for furniture and accessories. As the focal point, walls can draw attention away from awkward architectural features or furniture that you hope to replace. As a backdrop, walls emphasize the beauty of furniture and accessories.

When you are painting or wallpapering, get the most value from your decorating dollars by doing the work yourself.

Paint, the most widely used wall covering, is popular for several reasons. It is inexpensive and easy and quick to apply. You don't have to limit your color choice to a few paint chips of overworked tints. Just take swatches of drapery and upholstery fabric, or carpet samples with you, and have paint custom-mixed to match.

Keep in mind that light colors make a small room appear larger, whereas dark hues visually reduce the size of a large area. Light-colored ceilings, for example, add height to a room; dark colors lower them. And if rooms are small, they can be made to appear larger if the walls, doors, and woodwork are all painted the same color. Cut-up areas are less conspicuous if colors flow from one room to the next.

Besides the paint itself, be sure to have rollers and/or brushes, masking tape, patching plaster, and liquid sander and sandpaper. Also, use drop cloths to protect furnishings. Preparing for painting actually takes more time than the painting itself, but it is well worth the extra effort. Remove all doorplates and hardware, and sand all surfaces to remove wax and dirt. Remove all objects from walls, and use patching plaster to fill holes and cracks in the walls. If you are painting an entire room, paint the woodwork first, the ceiling second, and the walls last.

In the room below, the walls have been painted a neutral color to provide a subtle background for the wallpaper panel above the fireplace. Upholstery fabrics, decorative pillows, live plants, and other accessories repeat the same blues and greens that appear in the striking panel.

Three single rolls of wallpaper are all it took to cover the 9 x 10-foot wall in the dining area above. The luxurious wallpaper in brown, gold, and rust shades closely resembles a famous old jacquard fabric. The one wall that is papered performs decorative miracles in a white-walled room. This wall was covered for about $55; you can choose whatever price wallpaper you want.

Wallpaper, with its exciting patterns and colors, plays a vital role in home decorating today. It can completely alter the character of any room in your home, or create a new atmosphere, depending on the mood you desire.

Even the most fragile-appearing wallpapers have qualities that ensure long life and ease in hanging. Many of them are washable, pretrimmed, and prepasted. Some are even strippable and can be removed easily when it is time for a change in the decor.

Just as with so many other household things you buy, the more expensive designs are usually the most desirable. But with wallpaper, a large price-per-roll doesn't mean that you have to cross that desirable off your most-wanted list. Paper one wall, or hang one or two panels.

There is enough paper in a single roll to cover 35 square feet. Papers between 18 and 20½ inches wide come in double-roll bolts; wider papers, 28 inches wide, most often come in triple-roll bolts. This is to minimize waste.

WALL COVERINGS

In addition to the old stand-bys, paint and wall-paper, there are many other materials that can be used as wall coverings. The price, of course, depends on your choice of material and the size of the area to be covered. If you are a home-owner, you may decide that an expensive wall covering that will give many years of service and satisfaction is well worth the substantial initial investment. However, if you are a renter, you may have to consider limitations imposed by the building management.

Fabric is becoming increasingly popular as a wall covering. Because of the improved adhesives available, any fabric can be attached with liquid adhesive, hung with double-faced pressure-sensitive tape, or stapled to the wall.

The biggest advantage in using fabric to cover a wall, or walls, is that the same fabric can also be used for draperies, upholstery, cushions, or bedspreads. Use inexpensive fabrics such as cotton prints, gingham checks, mattress ticking stripes, denim, felt, or burlap for wall coverings, and you will save quite a lot of money.

Available, too, are more expensive, but not outlandishly priced, fabric wall coverings with an adhesive backing. All you have to do to apply these wall coverings is peel off the paper backing and press the fabric onto the wall. Felt, burlap, grass cloth, and many other textures and weaves are available in this type.

Cork on a wall brings the interest of natural materials indoors to you. Cork comes in nine-inch squares, or in panels, and runs from $1.60 to $2 per square foot. A single wall of cork, or just a panel above your fireplace, may be all you need to add warmth, comfort, and a unique touch to your room.

Wood paneling, factory-finished and low in cost, is so popular with home decorators that building supply dealers offer a wide selection in natural wood colors with molding and trim to match. Along with the beauty that mellow wood

Panels of fabric in a bold contemporary pattern run from the ceiling down the wall and over the bar surface in the living room below. Wallpaper or a vinyl-coated wall covering could serve the same function. If you use fabric, fasten it to the wall and bar with double-faced pressure-sensitive tape.

A vinyl wall covering in a rich, dark brown, snakeskin pattern provides a sharp color contrast for a light green carpet, plaid upholstery fabric with matching circular table cover, and a variety of accessories and wall hangings. Vinyl wall covering is easy to hang, washable, and with this type of overall design, there is no matching of patterns when cutting panels.

A wall that camouflages badly cracked plaster is made of rough, exterior cedar paneling. The paneling can be nailed directly to the wall or attached to a framing or fake stud wall to minimize nail holes in the room's wall. The neutral color of the paneling makes it an ideal background for a collection of colorful contemporary wall hangings, as pictured here.

Wallpaper panels can accessorize a stairway, too. Cut each panel in an appropriate design. You can apply the panels directly to the wall and then add the molding, or you can mount the paper on hardboard and hang each panel as you would hang pictures on a wall. Paint the molding strips to match some of the colors in the pattern before you fasten it to the panels.

You can add traditional charm to the most ordinary of walls by applying wallpaper panels in certain areas. Paint the molding that outlines each panel in an accent color. This same type of treatment could be adapted to any style of furnishings, or any color scheme, merely by choosing a wallpaper design that harmonizes with the furnishings in the room.

tones offer, paneling requires a minimum of up-keep and gives long years of service. The 4 x 8-foot prefinished panels are easy to install.

You can buy natural wood grains and colors to suit any room, any mood, or any style of furnishings. Wood paneling can be used for an entire room, a single wall, or simply a panel to provide accent. Regardless of whether your home is old or new, or whether the walls are in good or poor condition, paneling offers a once-and-for-all solution to wall decorating. Baked-on finishes eliminate the need for further finishing and are guaranteed to last a lifetime.

Tile that can be used as a decorative wall covering is available in many different types of materials. These cover a wide price range, but even the more expensive offerings can be used in a small area and produce an exciting decorative effect without too great an investment.

Metal wall tiles of gleaming solid copper, solid stainless steel, and several aluminum finishes come in 4¼-inch squares, packaged 12 to a carton. Those with built-in adhesive areas

inside each corner can be put up in minutes. A carton of 12 copper tiles costs about $3.25; stainless steel, about $2.25; and aluminum, about $1.55. Simulated tile or Florentine stone with a self-sticking back is also available and retails for about $3 for a package of six panels.

Parquet, at one time considered solely a type of wood flooring, makes a striking wall treatment, too. Parquet tiles of solid oak measure 9 x 9 inches and cost about 78¢ each. They are easy to apply with tile cement. For an 8 x 10-foot wall, the cost is less than $60, including cement, plywood, and edging for the base platform.

Fiber glass panels for walls simulate the look of natural materials such as brick, stone, or barn siding. They come in 4 x 8-foot sheets with a nailing lip around the edge for easy installation. The cost is about 50¢ per square foot.

Hardwood panels come in random-grooved, plastic-finished 4 x 8-foot sheets and cost about $9.50 each. These panels are washable, conceal cracked plaster, and are easy to apply to walls with finishing nails slightly countersunk.

Even a small room can grow big in decorating stature when a patterned fabric comes on the scene. To wake up the girl's bedroom below, an eye-focusing contemporary print cotton fabric is used to cover one wall and continue on across the ceiling. Colors taken from the print appear in the painted bed, bedspread, curtains, and wall poster. A generous amount of white magnifies the patterned print and contrasts with the stinging shrimp accent shade of accessories.

Rough, porous, concrete basement walls are ideal surfaces for textured paint—the rougher the better. To duplicate the wall treatment below, make cutouts from brick vinyl floor tiling and cement to the walls in a random pattern. Cover the bricks with a masking tape. Generously brush or roll textured paint onto the wall and, while paint is wet, pat with a wadded newspaper or coarse sponge. Work on the wall until you have a texture you like. When paint dries, remove tape.

Rugged burlap is a natural for the walls of a small child's room. Not only does it add texture and a sweep of color, but it can also serve as a giant-sized wall-to-wall bulletin board. You can get burlap in 18-inch wide rolls for about $2 a yard, with peel-off self-adhesive backing. More than a dozen bright-as-a-child colors are available. Before applying burlap, nail composition board to the wall above the chair rail. The extra thickness adds soundproofing.

Color, texture, pattern, and even some acoustical value are possible in a wall covered with indoor-outdoor carpet tiles. Especially easy to install are the foot-square tiles laid full size, or knife-cut for unique designs. This blue green wall scheme veers away from the usual checkerboard pattern. Tiles cut into pieces 3, 6, and 9 inches wide are used with full squares. To apply, use double-faced pressure-sensitive tape or a special adhesive for carpeting.

Vinyls, in a wide range of colors, patterns, and textures, are excellent materials for wall coverings. There are foam-, fabric-, and foil-backed vinyls; and plastic vinyls. They are washable, waterproof, and easy to apply.

(**1**) Foam-backed vinyl, with its smooth polish, conceals wall defects and irregularities, and has a sound-deadening quality, too. To install, stretch one panel on the wall at a time, tacking lightly for temporary holding. Fold back a wide edge and apply adhesive; then press firmly to the wall. Do this on all four sides. Remove the tacks when the adhesive is dry. Use a decorative band or molding to cover the seam.

(**2**) Fabric-backed vinyl, prepasted and strippable, is easy to hang and to remove. It peels off in one strip without steaming or scraping. These wall coverings won't streak, fade, or show wear, even after repeated scrubbings; they are reinforced with rayon for greater durability.

(**3**) Foil-backed vinyl is moistureproof, fadeproof, and scrubbable. You can hang it the same as wallpaper or buy it with self-adhesive backing. Foil-backed vinyl comes in 27-inch wide rolls and costs about 20¢ per square foot.

(**4**) Plastic vinyl has a self-adhesive backing, so all you have to do is cut the strips to fit, peel off the backing, and press strips down and smooth them out. Plastic vinyl comes in 18-inch wide rolls and costs about 50¢ per running yard.

Linoleum, in a bright color and pattern, can brighten up a dark, cheerless basement laundry room or a playroom when it is used on both walls and floor. Just cement the 12-foot width as seamless flooring and use the same pattern in the 9-foot width for the wall covering. Use plastic stripping to conceal any seams. Linoleum prices vary according to the quality.

Ceramic tile on the walls can make even a drab bathroom sparkle. Use a single color; or two or three colors in a block plaid pattern. First, cement the tiles to the wall, then complete the job by grouting. Ceramic tiles are 4¼ x 4¼-inches standard size and cost approximately 60¢ per square foot. The less expensive plastic tiles cost around 25¢ per square foot.

PERSONALIZED WALL TREATMENTS

You can achieve unusual and stunning wall treatments by making use of materials that don't ordinarily fall into the category of wall coverings. Whether your rooms have new walls, old walls, or problem walls, you can decorate them inexpensively and still achieve an individual look.

Paint, the simplest wall covering of all, can be given a personal touch and converted into a high-fashion background. You can accent a painted wall with borders; stenciled designs; motifs of fabric, vinyl, or wallpaper; or decorator tape. You can use wallpaper borders not only around the room at ceiling height, but also around window frames and doors, or as a dado at chair rail height. There are borders of varying widths with floral, striped, geometric, abstract, or trompe l'oeil designs in many combinations.

(1) Stencils. One method of adding interest to a painted wall is to use stenciled borders and designs. You can buy stencils in art supply stores or hobby shops, or you can make your own if you have a flair for art and design.

If you have an old-fashioned bathroom of Victorian vintage, flaunt it. The only cost involved in updating the one below was for paint, lumber for a shelf above the bathtub, and a wood theater light frame around the mirror. Use accessories to accent the color of the tub and the wall decoration.

It's the wallpaper, with its colorful, contemporary design, that makes the small guest powder room come alive. Add to this a sculptured tin mirror frame, a row of theater lights above it, and unique containers of crystal, silver, and bronze and you have a completely individual retreat for guests.

To break the monotony in a small room with white walls and ceiling, use a supersize graphic to cover a large area. Although this particular design exceeds the $100 figure, there are many designs and sizes that are less expensive. A wood strip is used at the top and bottom to moor the hanging to the wall.

A one-color stencil is the simplest, as there is an additional stencil for each additional color. Fasten the stencil to the wall securely with masking tape and use a stencil brush to paint in the design. When you remove the stencil, be careful not to smear the wet paint. The same stencil designs or borders that you use on the walls can also be used to decorate window shades, lamp shades, or pieces of furniture.

(**2**) Motifs. Another way to enliven painted walls is to cut out motifs of fabric, vinyl, or wallpaper and apply them to the walls in a pleasing arrangement. If you use fabric motifs, spray them with a clear lacquer or outline each design with clear nail polish before you cut them out. This will eliminate frayed edges. Use the same adhesive that you would for hanging wallpaper.

(**3**) Plastic tape. Decorator tape of plastic-coated cloth comes in a variety of vivid colors and is so simple to apply to humdrum painted walls. The ¾-inch width 8-yard roll costs about 70¢, and the 2-inch width 5-yard roll costs about $1. You can create your own patterns of stripes, plaids, or grillwork designs with this easy-on tape. Simply unroll it and press it on the wall; when it is time for redecorating, just peel off the tape. In an entrance hall, you can easily create a French Quarter-type atmosphere by using strips of black and gray tape to form a grillwork design. In a bathroom painted yellow, you might want to frame the vanity mirror and the tub area with stripes of orange and avocado, and then hang towels of the same shades.

(**4**) Aluminum tape. There is also a shiny aluminum tape that sells for about $1.70 per roll. In a contemporary room with tables and accessories of see-through glass, lucite, or shiny metal, you can strengthen the modern theme by covering one wall with shiny, wet-look vinyl and applying strips of the aluminum tape.

A trompe l'oeil wallpaper design is a wise choice if you want to visually enlarge a small area such as the narrow entrance hall at the right. In order to simulate the airy effect that this room has, carefully cut around portions of the design before applying it to the wall with wallpaper paste. You can strengthen the overall outdoor, summery feeling by fastening shutters, painted dark green, to the back of the entry door. In a small area, this type of wall treatment provides the total decorating scheme. It is not necessary to add pictures, accessories, or pieces of furniture, as the walls themselves are so dramatic that they capture the interest of all who enter.

The wall treatment below is a good example of how you can treat a problem wall. If you have a wall that has any cracks or crevices, first cover it with stain-resistant white cloth. Then attach narrow strips of wood in a latticework pattern, painted stark black, over the cloth wall covering. The lattice is notched at intervals to create a starlike pattern. The same lattice-work design is used at both windows to hold the curtains. Green foliage plants and a grass-colored shag carpet add contrast to the black and white wall treatment, and to the black and white checked upholstery fabric on the sofa-bedroom divider unit.

(5) Grillwork panels. Still another way to add pattern, texture, and color contrast to a wall painted a neutral color is to apply grillwork panels of plywood or hardboard directly on the painted wall. Unfinished panels can be purchased at building supply dealers in 6- to 8-foot lengths, and in widths from 15½ inches to 24 inches. Paint the panels to contrast with the color of the wall. For example, if you want a black and white color scheme, paint the walls white and cover one wall with grillwork panels painted black. Also paint one or more pieces of furniture black. Add some white accessories, a green plant, and several red accent pieces.

Bamboo. In a basement recreation room that is lacking in natural light, you can create a year-round outdoor atmosphere by covering the walls with bamboo. First, paint the concrete walls with a below-grade paint; then, measure to see how many feet you will need to go around the room. Use bamboo that has the strips woven with galvanized wire and comes in a 15-foot roll, 6 feet high. Unroll the bamboo as you go along, securing it to the wall here and there with concrete nails. An extra piece can be used at the base to act as a molding. Bamboo sells for $7.50 a roll.

It doesn't take any expensive materials or rare artistic talent to re-create the appearance of an art gallery in the small entrance hall at the left. All you need are a pair of sharp scissors, some clear varnish, and a few hours of your leisure time. Use color reproductions of paintings clipped from magazines, old books, or art folders. Group them in a pleasing arrangement, and glue them to the wall montage fashion. The same wall treatment has been extended to include the door panels and window panes. Finish the project by adding a protective coat of varnish. The black and white squares in the tile floor add a sharp contrasting note to the colorful walls.

If you have a very large collection of pictures, paintings, and prints, you can cover an entire wall, as shown in the picture below. This is an especially effective treatment when the walls are painted a neutral color. Use pictures of all sizes and shapes, all types of subject matter; with frames of various sizes, depths, and finishes. Plan your arrangement first by spreading the pictures on the floor and rearranging them until you are satisfied with the total grouping. In order to avoid too many holes in the wall, hang the lighter weight pictures with steel sewing needles driven into the wall on a slant.

Brick, that does not require the skill of a professional mason, can be used to cover a wall. These are kiln-fired bricks that are only ½ inch thick, and they are ideal for any wall where you want the beauty of brick, but you don't need the structural strength of conventional brick. All you have to do is to use mastic and install just as you would ceramic or plastic tile.

Cedar shakes and shingles offer still another type of material for a maintenance-free wall that features strong textures and grain patterns. These materials are easy to apply and, because they are attached to the wall individually, they can be arranged in whatever patterns, colors, and textural effects you desire. Cedar shakes and shingles can be stained any of the popular wood tones or decorator colors.

Mirrors will visually double the limited space of a small area such as a guest powder room or a tiny entryway. If you long for a mirrored wall, you can purchase 12 x 12-inch mirror tiles that are packaged six to a carton and that retail for about $9 per carton. And that's less than $100 for covering 60 square feet. Be sure to use special mirror mastic, since other adhesives might destroy the mirror's silvering. For a more expen-

Even though you have plain painted walls, you can convert them to take on the atmosphere of an English hunting lodge. First, install a framework of deep-stained or painted planks and beams, nailing them to the walls and ceiling. Then, protect wood with masking tape while you are applying the stucco with a wide brush or a stucco paint roller. Pat the freshly stuccoed wall with wadded newspaper to gain texture.

Outdoor reed screening gives the room above a subtle touch of Far East elegance at a surprisingly modest price. The natural finish of the wire-bound screening provides a quietly textured background that enhances any room. You can attach the screening to the back of a painted 2 x 4 and 2 x 2 frame. For an entirely different mood, you could stretch fabric instead of screening across the frame and staple it.

sive version, there are ½-inch square mirrors in 16 x 18-inch sheets that have a rubberized backing for easy handling. These tiny, glittering mirrors add a look of elegance; the cost is approximately $4 per square foot.

Woven veneers also make unique wall coverings. Available in walnut, birch, mahogany, rosewood, or teakwood finishes, they are plaited, laminated hardwood veneer strips in an open or closed design. These strips can be used alone or combined with felt or burlap panels. Panels retail for $12 to $15 for the 2 x 4-foot size, and $18 to $22.50 for 2 x 6-foot size.

In addition to the above ideas, there are many completely personal wall treatments you can put up that take little or no cash—just put your imagination to work. Why not cover a wall with sheet music or favorite record album jackets to please the music lovers in your family? If you want a touch of nostalgia, paper a wall with pages from old mail order catalogs. Posters come in all sizes, and many themes; you might like to mount circus posters in a child's room, or travel posters in a hallway. Also, there are maps of all sizes that you can use that add character to the walls of a den or library. In a game room, mount a dart board on one wall; or in a card game area, use playing cards on the wall. If there are bridge players in the family, arrange the cards like four 13-card bridge hands. If there are poker enthusiasts, arrange a "dead-man's hand" of aces and eights.

Use your ingenuity to conjure up ways to cover your walls so they reflect the interest and hobbies of your family. This is an opportunity to design an original background for furnishings.

These are the steps to follow for applying fabric panels to walls. (**1**) Spread the fabric on the floor and apply double-faced pressure-sensitive tape about ¼ inch from the edge on all four sides. Do not remove backing. (**2**) Hold the fabric to the wall at ceiling height and use a plumb line to create a vertical line on the side of the fabric. Draw a line on the wall with a pencil (**3**) Starting at the top, remove about 12 inches of backing and press the fabric firmly in place. Continue to remove backing, about 12 inches at a time, by pulling it toward you. Secure that part of the fabric and remove another 12 inches of backing. (**4**) Using the drawn line as a guide, press the fabric in place by removing the tape's backing in small sections. Repeat the process for the other side, pulling fabric taut to eliminate air pockets. Photo at right shows finished panel with matching bedspread.

It may not appear so, but the door above has got to be the easiest, quickest, and least expensive decorating project you could possibly attempt. The design is achieved simply by using two posters. The secret is to pick a poster that is symmetrical so the image will "mirror" when the bottom one is upside down. The door is a paneled door that has been painted the same neutral color of the walls and woodwork. Use adhesive to attach the posters to the door, and spray them with a clear lacquer to add a protective finish. It only takes a few dollars to buy similar posters.

HOW TO DECORATE DOORS

When decorating your home, don't forget the doors. In the past, they were very often totally unrelated to the complete home decorating scheme. Now, doors are included in decorating plans so that they harmonize with both the background colors and the style of furnishings in the room. Whether your doors are old or new, or solid or hollow-core, there are many ways to add decorative interest–most of them cost very little.

Doors can be painted to match or contrast surrounding walls, or covered with wallpaper, fabric, carpet, shiny vinyl, or grained leatherlike material. Flush doors take on a regal character when sculptured motifs and moldings are added. Paneled doors are given a new look when covered with a sheet of plywood. Whether your style of furnishings is traditional, contemporary, or country, doors can be redesigned so they are in tune with the room's decor.

Painted doors may be the perfect solution for you if your room is cut up, of if the doors are awkwardly placed. You may want to minimize them and let them fade into the background. One way to do this is by painting the doors and

A coat of paint and stainless steel strips (16 gauge, 6 inches wide) make these doors look new. Clean strips with lacquer thinner; stick them to doors with contact cement. Add walnut pulls made from ¾ x 9-inch scrap strips. Use ½-inch metal tube spacers between pull and door. Counterbore screws, plug holes with ⅜-inch dowel; then sand flush. Cost: $45.

woodwork the same color as the walls around them. When connecting rooms have different room colors, each side of the door should be painted to match the color of the corresponding room. The edges of the door should be painted to match the walls of the room into which the door swings. The doorjamb should match the edge of the door.

On the other hand, if you want to dramatize your doors and make them important decorative features, paint them to contrast with the walls. Choose a color that appears in the drapery or upholstery fabric, carpet, or wall hangings. With paneled doors, you may decide to paint the frame and panels different colors. If you do this, paint the narrow molding around each panel a striking contrast to enhance the color separation.

Distinctive doors can be achieved in many different ways, and most of the treatments are easy for the home decorator or handyman to do.

You can turn a drab door into a striking focal point by working out a smart basket-weave motif with two widths of plastic tape. First, paint the door any color you like with some semigloss enamel. Then, select two contrasting colors of tape, one ¾-inch and the other 1½ inches wide.

In a child's room, the door has been turned into a huge bulletin board by covering it with indoor-outdoor carpet tiles. There are two rows of charcoal gray tiles, and one of alternating light and dark blue tiles cut into three-inch widths. Spray adhesive on the back of each tile, and press onto the door. Cut tiles with a sharp scissors or knife. Cost: $18.

You can dramatize an old-fashioned paneled door if you give it a treatment similar to the one pictured above. First, remove the door from the hinges, and lay it flat. Remove all hardware, and use wood filler to repair any marred areas. Sand the entire surface, and repaint the door with fast-drying enamel. Here, the largest and most important areas were painted a bright red, and designs in several related colors were painted on the smaller areas. The molding was painted to simulate a frame for each large panel. Polish the hardware before refastening it. Cost: about $25.

The arched openings of these decorative doors are fitted with fine metal mesh to allow a free flow of light and air between a connecting bedroom and bathroom. Raised medallions, in tune with the elegant wallpaper, accentuate the styling of the doors.

In a hallway of dull, look-alike doors, why not hang an awning above your apartment door? Use striped canvas or any other firm fabric, and hang it on two curtain rods. Finish the scalloped edge with tassels and a tailored, narrow braid in a matching color.

A dark door can brighten a room when it's covered with shiny vinyl. This is an old paneled door covered first with a plywood panel. Glue vinyl fabric onto door with spray adhesive. Now, frame the plywood panel with wood molding that has been stained and finished before nailing and gluing it into place. Cost: $22.

Measure and mark the pattern on the door. Start in one corner and unroll the tape as you press it into place. Weave the strips over and under each other in the basket-weave design, and use a straightedge to keep the rows straight and at right angles. This type of decorative door treatment will cost only about $8.

With ready-carved trim, you can quickly make a run-of-the-mill door look formal and elegant. There are round, square, and rectangular sculptured designs in several sizes with matching border strips in narrow widths. Paint the door first; then apply stain, paint, or an antique finish to the trim. Glue or nail the moldings in place.

You can make interesting openwork doors for interior doorways by using reclaimed stairway spindles from old buildings. Make a framework of 1 x 2 pine, scaled to the size of the doorway, and mount the plywood sheets to lower end and top with a 1 x 2. Nail spindles to the frame.

Just by changing a wall covering or by altering a stock door, you can create a background that is subtle or bold. The wide range of materials that are easy to apply and care for makes decorating walls or doors an exciting project.

The colorful door below was painted in varying yellows, with wood picture molding and enameled pine battens added. Leaves were sawed from batting and hardwood; disks were sliced from broom handles and dowels. Undercoat, sand, and enamel all the pieces. Attach molding; glue small pieces. Cost: $20.

In the entrance hall above, the door has been painted to contrast with the antique gold walls. Handsome old posts, retrieved from a home that was being demolished, were added for architectural interest and painted the same color. The dull green color of the door and posts, and the antique gold walls, provide a mellow background that enhances the traditional accessories, lighting fixture, and furniture.

You can add a sparkle to a room's color scheme, add design interest, provide a pivotal point for the decor, or screen an architectural fault with window treatments that are practical and beautiful.

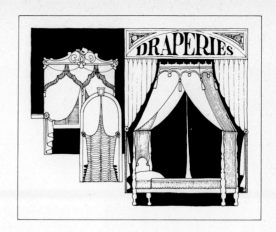

WINDOW TREATMENTS

Creating outstanding window treatments that reflect the decorating mood of your home is not as hard—or as costly—as you may think. A little effort on your part, and a knowledge of some basic guidelines will produce window treatments that are practical and attractive.

Regardless of the size, shape, and number of windows you have, you must first decide just what you want to accomplish with your window treatments. Remember that even though the primary function of a window is to provide ventilation, natural light, and an outdoor view, the ideal window treatment also affords privacy, adds beauty to the room, and complements the room's furnishings and colors.

If your windows overlook a scenic view, take advantage of the natural beauty and frame them as you would a painting. However, if you have an uninteresting or ugly view, conceal them. You can even use a window treatment to minimize structural oddities, to make radiators, air conditioners, and outmoded woodwork less conspicuous, or to camouflage problem windows—ones of different shapes and sizes.

Next, while you're thinking about which treatment to give your windows, don't forget to give just as much attention to choosing drapery hardware. Although standard traverse rods are still important in the home furnishings picture, decorative rods with coordinated tiebacks and holdbacks that give a simple window treatment a look of elegance are coming to the fore.

Lastly, use draperies, curtains, blinds, shutters, and window shades that add beauty to the room and its furnishings. These items are available in a wide range of colors and materials and can be used singly, or with two or more combined in a single window treatment.

If decorating windows seems like a gigantic undertaking, perhaps the ideas on the pages that follow will provide the inspiration you need to get started.

BUYING WINDOW TREATMENTS

Whether you are planning a total decorating project, or merely thinking of decorating windows to conform to your existing scheme, you can cut costs if you shop wisely. Most home furnishings departments carry a wide selection of draperies, curtains, blinds, shutters, and window shades in stock sizes. Unless you have windows of extremely unusual dimensions, you can avail yourself of these stock offerings. Usually, these are much less expensive than are those that must be special-ordered and custom-made to individual specifications.

Before you start shopping for these items, arm yourself with the accurate measurements for each window. If you find a picture in a book or magazine that illustrates the treatment you have in mind, take it with you, too.

The corner window above features a monochromatic color scheme. Ready-made, sheer, white batiste curtains blend the window with the walls on either side. Inexpensive, straight, ready-made draperies hang from a wooden pole. The white bands on the draperies and the tiebacks, and the white wooden rod and rings tie the brown and white color scheme together.

Sunlight filters through the ready-made sheer curtains at the right. The side panels are made by cutting in two a 2⅔-yard length of 48-inch wide drapery fabric. The panels hang from poles at the top, and are weighted down with poles at the bottom run through the casing. Paint the wooden poles, finials, and pole brackets the same color as the fabric panels.

Draperies and curtains, of almost every description, are available in a wide range of prices, sizes, and fabrics. Priced according to the quality of the fabric, and the size, they come in skillfully designed patterns, and in solid colors that range from subdued neutral tints all the way to bold and vivid shades. Lined draperies cost a little more than those that are unlined, but they have more body, afford greater privacy, and protect the fabric from the sun's rays. Lining also gives a more uniform appearance when viewed from the outside of the home.

Fabrics are constantly being improved by the introduction of new fibers and fiber blends. Also available are special finishes that add greater durability to the fabric, and that make draperies and curtains very easy to care for. Look for manufacturers' tags that tell just how to care for draperies and curtains.

Draperies and cafe curtains are combined in the eating area in the kitchen above. The multicolored cotton fabric is a pleasing complement for the cane-patterned vinyl wall covering that features the same shades of green that appear in the tile floor. Draperies drawn back during the day frame a beautiful view; closed at night, they ensure complete privacy.

The window treatment at the left is ideal for use in a room with contemporary furnishings if you have a view you wish to ignore or shut out. A smart, open-weave casement fabric is attached to brass rods at both the top and the bottom of the window; behind it there is a bottoms-up white opaque window shade that blots out the undesirable view outside.

Shutters and beads are combined in the window treatment above. The shutters have inserts of perforated hardboard (building supply dealers carry sheets of perforated hardboard in a variety of designs). The shutters can be painted whatever color you wish, or finished in a natural wood tone. Strands of beads come in many colors in opaque or gem-cut crystal versions and in wood. They are permanently fused to nylon cord, and can be cut to any length; and mounted on a bead track. Here, strands of round beads are interspersed with gem-cut crystal beads. This type of treatment requires a minimum of upkeep.

In the photo at the right, a splash of daring color at the kitchen window repeats the colors in the ceramic tile wall motif. The cotton fabric valance with its horizontal-striped pattern covers less than half the window. With the top uniformly pleated, it presents a tailored appearance. The stock shutters at the bottom half of the window are painted the same color as the walls on either side so that they won't detract from the decorative fabric above. Stock shutters can be purchased in many sizes with either movable or fixed louvers, or panel inserts. The price of the valance and shutters is about $48.

Blinds, shutters, and shades combine function and beauty and are available in an endless array of styles and colors. Any one of them can provide a complete window treatment, or can be used with draperies, curtains, valances, or cornices. How you use them will depend on the style of furnishings of the room you are decorating, and the amount of money you spend.

Blinds come in a variety of styles and materials, and adapt well to new and glamorous decorative treatments. The venetian blinds of yesteryear have been replaced by new versions that have slim slats in laminated colors. They are available with horizontal or vertical slats in wood, steel, or aluminum. There are also bamboo and matchstick blinds that can be left plain, or painted; trimmed with fringe, braid, yarn, ribbon, fabric, or colorful vinyl tape.

Shutters may seem like an expensive item, but their long life and ease of maintenance make them a wise long-term investment. In addition to their decorative interest, they can disguise problem windows, and conceal air conditioners and radiators. They allow maximum flexibility in light control and ventilation and, at the same time, ensure privacy. You can buy shutters in painted or natural wood finishes, or unfinished. They come in a wide range of stock sizes, or can be ordered for windows of unusual dimensions.

Panels are designed with movable or fixed louvers; or with cane, mesh, solid panel, stained glass, perforated hardboard, or fabric inserts.

Window shades that fit windows of all sizes, and that suit any decorating mood—traditional, country, or contemporary—can also be purchased. There are four basic types from which to choose: the pull-down shade; the Austrian shade; the Roman shade; and the bottoms-up shade. All of these come in plain or textured material that is either opaque or translucent. The opaque material ensures complete room-darkening qualities; the translucent material allows light to filter through. Shades come in striped, patterned, or solid colors that range all the way from the most unobtrusive, subtle, neutral tints to high-fashion, vivid decorator shades. They can be simply tailored; accented with a decorative trim; or have a custom-look with shaped hems, scalloped borders, and matching cornices.

Austrian and Roman shades are not attached to shade rollers, but are regulated with a cord, rings, and a pulley. The Austrian shade is shirred and draped when lowered or raised; the Roman shade falls into pleats when it is raised.

Bottoms-up shades are mounted from the bottom of the window and are regulated by tracks on either side. This mounting provides flexibility in light control, ventilation, and privacy.

The window treatment above blends the entire window wall into the decorating scheme. The white vinyl decorative shades with scalloped borders are accented with braid trim and shade pulls. The same curved design is repeated in the cornice. Build a cornice of plywood around the whole window area and under the windowsills, too, and cover the sills with a shelf. Then, fasten in solid wood columns to cover the spaces between the windows. Cover the end wall and cornice with black burlap. Apply strips of green burlap to the cornice uprights. Paint sills or cover with plastic laminate. Cost: $88.

This kitchen window treatment offers the ultimate in light control. You can have as much color, view, light, and privacy as you desire. Choose the combination of colors that you want, and have them cut to size at a shade shop. Be sure to measure the width carefully when you order them. The shades should be 12 inches longer than the window itself. These are easy to install, and you can change the color combination at any time for exciting variations. You can choose any combination of colors that reflects the overall decorating scheme. Here, the same colors are repeated in the accessories on the counter. Cost: $47.

CUSTOMIZING WINDOW SHADES

The elegant, expensive-looking window treatment you admire is not out of reach if you buy stock window shades and add your own trim to give them an elegant custom appearance. This is easy, even for the inexperienced decorator.

You can trim a shade with a precut, prescalloped, self-adhesive fringed skirt merely by pressing it onto the shade. And you can do this for about half the cost of a custom-made shade with a scalloped border. Or you can add one or more rows of press-on braid or fringe in matching or contrasting colors to create a border effect that harmonizes with furnishings in the room.

There are so many eye-catching, low-cost ideas you can use. Designs can be appliqued on shades and valances. Cut out motifs or borders

from vinyl-coated wall covering or tightly woven fabric and glue them firmly in place on the shade. Before cutting a fabric design, spray the fabric on the back side with an acrylic spray or outline it with a coat of colorless nail polish. This will prevent the edges from raveling. Smooth each design carefully so that there are no air bubbles between the shade and the applique. After the glue is dry, protect the designs with another coat of acrylic spray.

You don't have to create original designs when stenciling window shades. You can buy stencils in art supply shops. If you cut your own, let wall covering or fabric patterns used elsewhere in the room guide you. Use textile paint, and apply it with a stencil brush held in an upright position. With a circular motion, work the paint into the stencil motif. After it has dried, iron it.

In the living room below, a decorative valance has been added to top off a wall of inexpensive, semi-translucent, floor-length draperies. A board, covered with fabric, has been mounted above the plain draperies to support the tailored, tasseled hangings that are made of the same bold-patterned fabric that appears in the sofa in front of the windows.

In the dining area below, an applique border taken from an upholstery fabric has been applied to Roman shades and matching valance. To keep raw edges from raveling when appliqueing, paint cutting line on reverse side of fabric with colorless nail polish. The scallops in the design coordinate the shades and valance with the furnishings and colors in the room.

The window treatment above has a "special order" look that is very simple and inexpensive to duplicate. A white stock shade of translucent material is trimmed with a precut, prefringed skirt that is self-adhesive and can be readily pressed on in minutes. The ready-made draperies feature a white fern design on a black background. A black-seated Chippendale chair is painted a daring orange. Black and white in small doses reappear in accessories throughout the room.

Wall-to-wall draperies, in three shades of brown on white, conceal uneven plaster. The smart white window shade has a distinctive texture, and the applique designs cut out from the drapery fabric add flavor and give the design theme special continuity. Both draperies and shade are hung from the ceiling to give the old-fashioned windows height they don't really have. An exposed radiator under the window fades out behind a homemade screen covered with shade cloth.

A tiny entrance hall-dining area gains importance by being ingeniously unified with a handsome, stenciled, oriental design. The pattern is used as a border on the oyster white window shade that matches the wall color. The same motif is run all around the window to create a decorative frame, and is continued with three-dimensional effect as an interesting dado. This cleverly scaled design continuity creates a complete room scheme with the stroke of a paint brush.

For a no-sew window treatment in the handsome living room below, a refreshing floral print fabric is laminated to the window shade. The shade, specially designed for laminating, is adhesive-coated and heat-sensitive. You can "iron on" almost any fabric you choose. The heat from the iron activates the adhesive. The shade is trimmed with a border of pressure-sensitive nylon velvet ribbon—one row of black, one of yellow. Fabric is repeated in upholstered cushions.

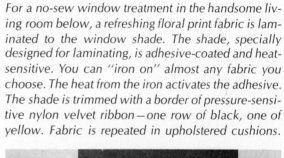

A smashing striped cotton fabric, laminated on a vinyl room darkening shade, establishes a lively note in a boy's room. The wide window is framed with a semicircle of blue vinyl laminated on plywood that accents the blue stripe in the shade fabric. The same fabric is used to cover throw pillows.

NOVEL WINDOW TREATMENTS

In addition to the conventional window treatments featured in the preceding pages, there are many other ways to give your windows character and individuality. On the pages that follow, there are numerous examples of novel ideas in photos, captions, and text that should inspire you to create your own window "architecture."

If you are covering windows with draperies or curtains, and are keeping one eye on the budget, remember that it is more effective to use an inexpensive fabric generously than it is to skimp on expensive material. Inexpensive denim, that hangs with ample fullness, is very often more beautiful than costly damask that is skimpy. It isn't the price that you pay for the fabric that's most important, but how you use the fabric.

Sheets and towels are ideal fabrics to use when you want to create unusual window treatments. For beauty, practicality, and economy, they're hard to match. New designs feature stripes; plaids; and geometric, floral, and jungle patterns, plus solid colors. Sheets come in widths up to 108 inches, or double the width of most regular drapery fabric. There are no seams and no matching patterns to worry about. Better yet, sheets are preshrunk and ready-hemmed. Besides, the permanent press qualities enable you to launder them in the washing machine, dry them in the dryer, and rehang without pressing.

You can use no-iron sheets to make draperies, curtains, valances, dust ruffles, bed canopies, even bedspreads. If you have shutters with fabric panel inserts, you can use a patterned sheet to make the fabric panels. In a bathroom, you can use towels to make draperies and a matching shower curtain. In a child's room, which is the center of a lot of action, use sheets with a circus, a jungle, or a nautical theme for draperies and matching bedspread. Only the slightest amount of needlework expertise is necessary to create these decorating items from sheets and towels.

Other fabrics, such as sturdy striped mattress ticking, unbleached muslin, denim, terry cloth, and checked gingham, also lend themselves to inexpensive and interesting window treatments. Simple, pleated draperies of unbleached muslin can coordinate all of the furnishings in a room if you trim them with rows and rows of rickrack and braid in colors that match upholstery fabric, carpets, wall coverings, and accessories.

Tailored draperies of bright red sailcloth add sparkle to a room with neutral walls when they are teamed with red and white striped window shades, and surrounded with ceiling-high bookshelves painted the same cheery red. Charcoal gray and white striped mattress ticking, trimmed with bands of black, white, and bright yellow braid or ball fringe, is a popular choice for either draperies or cafe curtains. Use the same black, white, and yellow in furnishings and accessories elsewhere in the room; add a few live, green plants for a sharp contrast.

In a girl's room that has wall covering with pink flowers and green leaves, use pink and white checked gingham draperies, bedspread, and canopy. Repeat the same pink and green in

In the small den-guest room below, the single, wide window has a yellow burlap shade with shaped hem that matches the lines of the cantonierre around the frame. Both are trimmed with brush fringe. By using a lower tier of burlap cafe curtains, and covering the wall in the same fabric, the room gains unity, spaciousness.

Convert a brass headboard into an ornate cornice. Construct a plywood back plate with side projections, fasten to wall at ceiling height. Attach a ⅜-inch brass rod and shirr on draperies. Unscrew and remove side posts from headboard, invert, and screw to plywood back plates. Paint back plate; attach rods. $20.

In the kitchen above, one end of the room that has been reserved for eating, has a distinctive window treatment. The louvered shutters are painted pink to match the color of the table and chairs. The half-draperies above the shutters are the same color as the background in the wall covering, and the wide bands of fabric have the same pattern as the wall covering.

painted furniture pieces, and accessories that appeal to a young girl. For a boy's room, you can use care-free denim or terry cloth for draperies, matching bedspread, and pillows.

A colorful Roman shade can be made of almost any fabric that has a firm weave. Cut fabric to the size of the window, allowing 1½ inches for each side hem. For horizontal tucks, add about two inches to the length of the shade. You can buy special Roman shade tape. It has small plastic rings every few inches, and will save sewing time. Insert a heavy cord through tape rings so the shade can be raised or lowered. Attach the shade to the window frame. Run the cords through the top rings, bring the lines to one end, hook through eye, and tie.

Window trims can add the finishing touch to an otherwise ordinary window treatment. With the wealth of braids, borders, and tapes available, it is easy to customize draperies or curtains you make yourself, or ready-mades you buy.

If you want a trim, contemporary treatment that dresses a bedroom window in style, try a panel of brightly colored striped linen. Stretch the fabric on a lightweight wood framework, and suspend it on a ceiling track. You can slide the fabric to one side to free the window, or you can completely cover it if you want privacy.

Materials other than fabric can also be used for window treatments. If you have a bathroom, entryway, or stairway-landing window that is awkwardly placed and looks out on a view you would like to ignore, why not cover the window with colored glass? Buy chunks of colored glass from a glass company, break them with a hammer into small pieces, then glue the pieces to the window, in a random pattern with clear epoxy. It shouldn't cost more than $11 for the glass.

Strands of beads create a sparkling window treatment that allows light to enter and air to circulate. Individual beads are bonded to nylon cord which can be cut to fit any window height.

Wall-to-wall burlap gives unity to the bedroom grouping above. For the window treatment, putty-colored burlap was stapled on hinged plywood panels. Each panel is edged in gimp to give a finished look. The same burlap was used to cover the wall around the windows. The desk table in front of the windows was treated to a speckle-finish that matches the burlap color, and a painted stripe that matches the gimp.

An ugly, wrong-sized window has been camouflaged by using shutters. A frame that extends just a few inches from the wall was built to enclose the window area. Shutters with fabric inserts were hung in the frame to create an interesting and attractive facade while hiding an architectural flaw. The fabric adds pattern to the decor, yet requires only a minimum of sewing—hemming sides, casings at top and bottom.

For a teen-age boy's room, the black and white color scheme teamed with vibrant green makes a great setting. The black and white cane pattern of the laminated shades is repeated on the walls below the windows. The shutters between the windows, and at the lower half of each, add unity.

If you have a kitchen window with a view you want to hide, this may be the answer for you. Buy a piece of colored plastic with an embossed pattern and have it cut exactly to size to fit in the window frame over the glass panes. Cut a piece of plywood in the design of your choice, paint it, and mount over the plastic.

The window treatment is the big attraction in this bright and colorful bay window dining area. First, measure your windows for rods; then, mount the hardware and rods. Now, measure accurately for cafe curtains and valances. For pleated valance, and adequate fullness of cafe curtains, make sure the width of the fabric is twice the length of the rods. Next, select a complementary colored cotton or linen fabric for the window shades. Cut the fabric to the size of the shade rollers, and 12 inches longer than the length of the windows. Iron fabric, and mount on shade rollers; spray with plastic coating. Cost: about $95.

You can beautify a series of windows by installing decorative, fabric-covered plywood panels. Start by stapling padding to the fronts of the panels. If the panels show from the outside when the draperies are open, staple the fabric to both sides. Wrap the entire panel in fabric and staple along the edge where the ends meet. Fasten panels in place with metal corner angles screwed to the backs of panels at top and bottom. Screw angles to floor and ceiling. You might want to repeat the fabric pattern elsewhere in the room as was done here. Cost: about $36.

A valance-drapery combination frames a scenic view in the long set of kitchen windows above. The valance of white vinyl-coated fabric has a tailored, scalloped border trimmed with narrow black braid. The draperies of yellow cotton fabric are accented with a border of black and white braid. Add yellow accessories.

If your sewing skills are negligible, and your budget is taxed to the limit, this must be the most effective window treatment you can choose. Buy enough brightly colored felt to cover the window (this should cost less than $3), two dowel rods, and two cup hooks to support the top rod. You can simplify this still further by using two suspension-type rods that need no hardware for installation. Create an openwork design that harmonizes with your decor. Draw the designs on the felt, and use your scissors to cut them out. Lastly, hem the top and bottom, and mount the finished article on rods.

Roman shades in brown, rust, and gold cover the floor-to-ceiling windows in the dining area at the left. Windows flood the room with natural light and expose a beautiful garden view. When the Roman shades are pulled high, the outdoor view is revealed; when they are drawn at night for privacy, they cover the entire wall and resemble a fabric wall covering. The gold is repeated in the chair cushions, table linens, dishes, crystal, and centerpiece of garden flowers. The tiffany-type hanging fixture and a wall hanging echo the beige tones in the fabric.

Cover unsightly windows with 1 x 2-inch light wood frames with fabric panels. Center panel is fixed; end panels open to provide access to windows. Use airy, openweave fabric. Make center frame first, and tack or staple fabric over back of panel. Fasten wood strips against sidewalls to hinge movable shutters on. Cover frames with fabric and hang with butt hinges.

Cornices and valances add a great deal to the appearance of a room, and give a custom-look to a window treatment. They are usually combined with draperies, curtains, blinds, shutters, or shades. For a hand-carved effect, sculptured moldings and motifs can be applied to cornices before painting. If you want a padded effect, build the cornice of inexpensive lumber and tack, or staple a layer of foam rubber or cotton batting over the cornice before you cover it.

While a cornice is a shallow, boxlike structure usually made of wood, a valance is a strip of fabric, leatherlike vinyl, shade cloth, or canvas that hangs above a window. The valance may be straight or scalloped; draped, pleated, or shirred. Many types of attractive valances are quite easy to make; just make a casing at the top and thread it on a curtain rod. Cut the border in whatever design you prefer, and accent the valance with trim of braid or fringe.

Boldly patterned panel screens make this window treatment a winner. Four panels of plywood, 18 inches wide and 7 feet tall, are hinged in pairs. A striking fabric is then stretched over the panels and stapled to the back. For added luxury, pad the panels with cotton batting or polyurethane foam. Use panels over inexpensive ready-made sheers. Cost: about $67.

You can adapt these gay Roman shades in the fabric of your choice. You'll need fabric equal to 1½ times the window height. (If your windows are 3½ feet tall, you'll need 5¼ yards.) On reverse side, stitch ready-made Roman shade tape vertically at 10-inch intervals. Scallop the shade and valance, and trim both with decorative binding and tassels. Cost: about $24.

You can use medium-weight, plain white cotton duck for the novel Roman shade, matching valance, and draperies shown in the breakfast area below. The valance and shade have a smart, scalloped border. Add a patriotic punch, as well as a sharp color contrast, with colorful red and navy braid on white for the shade trim, and the drapery tiebacks. Cost: about $24.

If you'd like to light up a gloomy corner, why not combine the virtues of both a window and a tapestry? Fluorescent lights glow through printed fabric to create this effect. Frame is made of 1 x 4-inch pine, piano-hinged to wall. This is an original batik, priced at $75, but you can buy an interesting fabric panel for about $5 a yard. Cost: $20, plus fabric.

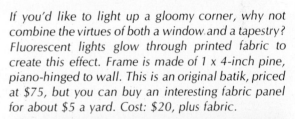

There's something new underfoot, and it's a whole new and exciting assortment of floor coverings. New decorating ideas will spring into action when you explore the wide, wide world of carpeting, area rugs, and resilient flooring. You can develop a decorating theme from the floor covering.

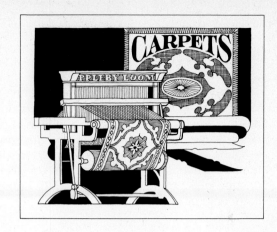

FLOOR COVERINGS

Floor coverings are no less important than any of the other major furnishings in your home. So, why not make floors and floor coverings an integral part of your decorating scheme? Properly chosen, these items will set the pace for the furnishings you already have, and for those you hope to acquire.

These floor coverings fall into basic categories: wall-to-wall carpeting, room-sized rugs, area rugs, tiles, hard-surface sheets, and natural wood.

If you're a home owner, wall-to-wall carpeting, or a good-quality room-sized rug is probably the best overall investment for you. But, since you'll rarely be able to buy this type of carpeting for less than $100, shop around for an area rug. For those of you who are trying to adhere to a limited budget, one or more area rugs will serve you just as well as wall-to-wall carpeting or a room-sized rug. You can choose from a wide selection of accent rugs—hooked, shag, Rya, felt, crocheted, and needlepoint.

In recent years, indoor-outdoor carpets and rugs have become fashionable in every area of the home because of their versatility. These carpets and rugs come in plain, textured, tweed, and tufted weaves that are long-wearing and highly fade-resistant.

Even old and scarred floors can be rejuvenated if you're willing to give them a little attention. Make the most of their natural beauty by sanding, staining, and waxing them. Then, if you wish, top them with an accent or area rug.

Also available is an exciting array of resilient floor coverings. No matter which pattern you're looking for—brick, terrazzo, stone, decorator colors, wood-grain, Spanish and Moorish designs—you'll find it in resilient floor coverings.

With all of the new patterns, textures, colors, fibers, materials, and methods of manufacturing available today, your chances of getting a serviceable floor covering at a price that is well within your budget are better than ever before.

62

BUYING FLOOR COVERINGS

You may think that buying a floor covering for less than $100 is an impossible chore, but don't despair. Realistically, you won't be able to carpet a large room wall-to-wall for this small amount, but there are many other ways to solve the floor-covering problem. You can use accent or area rugs, carpet remnants, indoor-outdoor carpeting, or resilient flooring.

If yours is an older home that is already carpeted, but because the carpeting can still withstand another year or more of wear, you can't in all honesty justify the cost of replacing it, add an accent rug. If the carpeting is one of the neutral shades of beige or gray, add new life to the room with an area rug that has a bold pattern and vivid colors. On the other hand, if the carpeting is a bright shade, add textural interest with a deep shag rug, or a fur or fake fur rug.

A black and white houndstooth check area rug adds interest to a room furnished with country-style antiques and reproductions. The black and white theme is repeated in the window treatment, and contrasts sharply with red walls and accessories. The 4 x 6-foot all wool rug retails for about $75.

A budget-priced, off-white, fake fur area rug provides a handsome accent in the living room above. A convincing double for the wool imports from Greece, it is a blend of synthetic fibers and has a sturdy knitted backing with a nonskid latex coating.

This unreal fur area rug, which sells for about $20 for the 30 x 54-inch size, and about $60 for a 5 x 7-foot size, has a silky texture and distinctive markings of cross fox pelts. It is highly resistant to wear and soil, and it may be washed or dry cleaned.

An accent rug can star in many roles. Because they come in many sizes, and in a variety of shapes—round, oval, square, rectangular, free-form—area rugs can be the connecting link of a conversational grouping, can brighten up a dim corner of a room or a tiny hall, or can set apart a dining area from the rest of the room. Accent rugs not only come in different sizes, but there are also modern and traditional patterns.

If yours is a room with country-style furnishings, treat it to one of the number of hooked rugs; for a traditional room, lay down a rug with a regal oriental pattern; and in a room with contemporary furnishings, accent it with a shag rug of a deep pile, or a fur or fake fur rug. For a breakfast room, or an indoor-outdoor room, use hand-woven rugs of rugged sisal-like fiber in lacy patterns. Their natural color complements

any color, and the price for a circular one four feet in diameter is about $12.

If you've just invested most of your savings in a down payment for a new home, and you're staring at bare floors that need immediate attention, purchase some inexpensive indoor-outdoor carpet tiles that can be used in any room of the house. These tiles are very easy to install and need no adhesive or underpadding to keep them firmly in place. They are quite easy to care for, and range in price from $3 to $5 per square yard. Also available are nylon shag tiles that come in a host of decorator colors. The 12 x 12-inch tiles have a rubber backing and retail for about 95¢ each. You can even buy carpet tiles with printed, tufted patterns that retail for about 75¢ per tile. If one of these tiles happens to get damaged, simply remove and replace with a new tile.

The delicate, brown-to-creamy white shadings of this fake fur area rug closely resembles sheared Canadian beaver. Because of its velvety warmth, it is ideal for a bedside rug. It harmonizes well with any style of furnishings, and is easy to maintain.

This fake fur rug, an amazing likeness of precious red fox pelts, is especially suited to the contemporary furnishings in the room below. It has a luxurious look, and is a silky blend of 80 percent Verel modacrylic and 20 percent acrylic yarns.

The area rug above is made from carpet samples without any sewing at all. Cut a piece of burlap at least two inches larger all around than the size you want the finished rug. Cut the rug samples to size. Then, glue the pieces to the backing. When it is dry, cut away excess backing. Cost: $18.

Carpet remnants and samples offer many opportunities to create interesting floor coverings with a minimum of expense. You may have to do a little searching, but you can find carpet samples priced from 50¢ on up. Remnants and ends of bolts are very often priced at a fraction of the original per-yard cost. Put your imagination to work, and figure out what design is best suited to your style of furnishings. Another incentive for creating this type of rug is that you are in no way limited by stock sizes; just measure the dimensions of the area that you want to cover, then cut the remnants or samples to fit.

Infinite variety is yours when you make a rug of carpet samples or remnants. You can select these remnants in various tints and shades of one or more colors and, if you want a uniform thickness, in the same texture and weave. If

you're trying to achieve a totally unique rug design, take advantage of the contrasts by combining many different textures, weaves, colors.

You may experience some difficulty finding the exact carpet colors you want. But don't despair. Cut some of the samples and dye them yourself. First, test a small piece of carpet in the dye solution to see how it absorbs the color, then wet the pieces to be dyed before immersing them in the dye bath. Afterwards, rinse the carpet with warm water and spin in the washing machine. Let the carpet pieces dry overnight before cementing in place on the burlap backing.

When you make rugs of this type, be sure to use a good-quality, heavy burlap for the backing. Buy enough so that it is a few inches longer and wider than the size you want the finished rug to be. Use carpet cement to glue the carpet pieces to the burlap backing, and trim away excess burlap backing after glue is thoroughly dry.

To cut carpet samples and remnants, always use a sharp knife and cut on the back side. Draw your lines first, using a straightedge to guide you so that each piece will be accurate. This is especially important, if you are cutting unusual shapes, such as triangles or hexagons. When each piece is to be identical, ensure uniformity by making a cardboard pattern to cut around.

To make a bordered area rug, look around for a remnant about six by nine feet for the center, and another about three by nine feet for the border. Cut the border piece into four equal strips. Keep two strips in the nine-foot length, and cut the other two in six-foot lengths. Cut the ends of each strip so they will form mitered corners to fit the edges of the center piece. Glue the center piece and the border strips to a burlap or canvas backing. This type of rug can have either a solid color center with a contrasting solid color border, or a patterned, striped, or plaid center with a solid color border that matches one of the colors in the center.

For a hexagonal rug using four colors, cut a cardboard pattern six inches long. Then cut six pieces of one color, seven of another, and 12 each of the two remaining colors. Starting with a hexagon in the center, glue the pieces to the burlap backing with carpet cement. Then, glue out from the center, completing each row. When the last row is finished, trim the edges of the hexagons with strips of one of the colors, and add a one-inch strip for a border.

Most of the carpet samples used in making the area rug above were dyed to get the vibrant colors. Mix the dye solution in a stainless steel or enamel pan and keep it simmering on a burner. Wet the pieces to be dyed before immersing them in the solution. Rinse with warm water, and spin in washing machine; let dry overnight. Cut samples in the design of your choice, glue them to burlap backing. Cost: about $22.

Leftover carpet scraps of many textures, weaves, colors, and sizes have been combined in the area rug below. Lay the scraps out on the floor and arrange, and rearrange them until you have worked out a design that pleases you. Then, cut a piece of heavy felt a little larger than the finished rug size and glue the carpet scraps to the backing. Trim away the excess backing and the area rug is ready to use.

The Rya method of making spectacular area rugs, wall hangings, and pillows originated in the Scandinavian countries. There's only one stitch to master, and a loom or a frame is unnecessary. The only materials needed for these rugs are heavy foundation fabric, wool, yarn, and needles.

RUGS THAT YOU CAN MAKE

For those of you who want the ultimate in individuality, and are willing to invest some time and effort, there are many types of rugs that you can make yourself. You can be as selective as you desire about colors and patterns because you are not limited by ready-made offerings. There are hooked, Rya, felt, braided, crocheted, and needlepoint rugs that can provide a dramatic accent to your furnishings. Besides, there is a great feeling of accomplishment when you create something that is beautiful and useful.

Hooked rugs can be made two different ways: one is to use the old-fashioned hook that is actually a large steel crochet hook fastened to a wood handle; the other is an automatic rug hooker. With the first type, you work from the right side and pull each loop through the burlap backing to the height you desire. With the automatic rug hooker, you work from the back and guide the needle while you crank it like an egg beater. It hooks up to 500 uniform loops a minute, and can be adjusted to three different loop heights. The needle sells for $6.95. With the automatic hook, use three- or four-ply worsted yarn. With the conventional hook, use either the same type of wool rug yarn, or cut up discarded wool garments and blankets into narrow strips. This is the method that thrifty pioneer women used in years past.

You can buy kits that contain all the materials needed for making hooked rugs. The kit for a 24 x 40-inch rug costs about $25, for a 3 x 5-foot size it costs about $40, and for a 4 x 6-foot size it runs about $70. Each kit has the burlap backing, wool yarn, and easy-to-follow instructions.

Creating your own designs is fun. Buy burlap by the yard and use either wool rug yarn, or narrow strips of wool material. Fasten the burlap to a sturdy wooden frame, stretching the burlap taut as you fasten it. Ready-made frames are available that can be adjusted to accommodate rugs of any size or shape. After the hooking is completed, fold the edges of the burlap underneath, and hem it by hand.

An easy way to seal the loops and loose ends, and also to make a nonslip backing, is to apply a coat of latex backing with a paint brush. Then, let the backing cure for 24 hours.

Rya rugmaking is an art that originated in the Scandinavian countries. All the materials that are needed—the heavy foundation fabric, wool yarn, and needles—can be purchased in kit form. Looms and frames are unnecessary. You can put the rug in your lap while you're working, but because the rug becomes too heavy to hold comfortably, it's easier if you work on a tabletop. You need only master the simple lockstitch, which you make with three strands of yarn, following the pattern stamped on the backing. As you proceed, stop from time to time to cut the loops of yarn, giving the rug a slightly uneven nap. Finish the rug by hemming the outer edges. Prices range from $40 for a 28 x 44-inch size, to $100 for a 4 x 6-foot size.

The 33 x 50-inch hooked rug, which features a charming little girl with flowers, can be purchased in a kit. The kit contains the design stamped on burlap, an ample supply of wool yarn to complete the rug, and a rug hook you'll need to do the rug by hand. You will have to buy some liquid latex to coat the back of the finished rug. The kit sells for about $40.

The rug below, with its storybook motif, is especially appropriate for a child's room. Cut the designs out of felt, and then applique them to a white felt background. Be careful not to stretch the felt while you are working on it. Trim the edge with a border of heavy-duty ball fringe. Felt comes in a wide range of dramatic colors that are brilliant and beautiful.

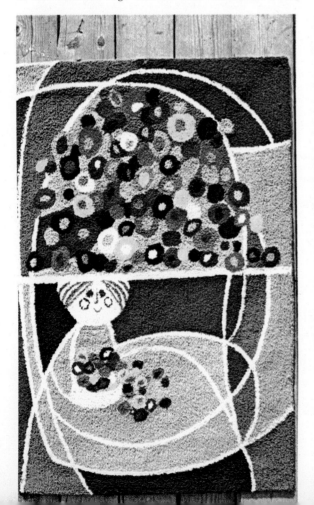

The glowing hooked rug below will go beautifully in front of a hearth, in a foyer or family room, or on a porch. These sturdy rugs wear well, even with heavy traffic. The rich tones of yellow, bronze, gold, and white accent the dramatic olive, and add depth to the rug. Available in kit form, this rug comes in either 51 x 67 inches at about $70; or 28 x 43 inches, priced at about $25. Kit includes stamped burlap, wool yarn, and instructions.

The area rug above is simple to braid and to assemble when you use strips of 72-inch wide felt. Pick three or four color-coordinated shades; repeat one of the colors in felt tassels. Lace the braided pieces together with a bodkin or blunt needle strung with heavy thread. Spray rug with stain repellent. Cost: about $9.

The felt area rug above complements the beauty of parquet floors. Combine felt motifs in shades of gold, white, and light and dark green with contrasting touches of mandarin orange and red. Applique designs on a gold felt background and edge with thick fringe. Use a rubber rug pad underneath.

Felt area rugs can easily be created—either by hand or by machine—by anyone who can thread a needle. These relatively inexpensive rugs can be made in a variety of colors to your own design. For the rug base, it is preferable to use a fairly heavy felt (50 percent or more wool is best). Applique the designs directly to the background. For machine appliqueing, set the machine for full width of satin-stitch and use heavy-duty mercerized threads related in color to the fabric. If appliqueing by hand, use a whip-stitch or buttonhole-stitch. Trim the edges with cotton or wool fringe that overlaps the raw edges.

Braided rugs can be made of narrow strips of felt; or wool, cotton, silk, or a wide variety of synthetic fabrics. When you sew the braided strips together in the round or oval design of your choice, lay them on a flat surface so that the finished rug will not curl up when laid. Use a heavy-duty carpet thread for sewing the rug together, and work from the back side. Join the strips together securely, and finish the rug by coating the underside with a latex backing.

Crocheted rugs can be made of wool or cotton rug yarn; or any type of wool, cotton, silk, or synthetic material that is pliable, easy to work with, and resists fraying. If you are using material rather than yarn, first experiment by cutting strips of the material in several different widths, and crochet a few stitches to see which width produces the thickness that you want. For example, a heavy material should be cut in narrower strips than should a lightweight fabric. But with either material or yarn, if you are crocheting a round or oval rug, increase stitches around the curves so the rug will lay flat. These rugs help create a homey atmosphere in a room with antique or country-style furnishings.

Needlepoint rugs are made with the same stitch as other needlepoint, except that the rug canvas has a much coarser screen. Needlepoint rug yarn is a great deal heavier than is the regular needlepoint yarn used for pillows, wall hangings, and chair seats. Needlepoint rug kits contain all the necessary materials. These rugs are compatible with traditional furnishings.

RESILIENT FLOORS

Manufacturers, continually on the alert to meet the needs of the public, are very much aware of the growing number of weekend handymen. As a result, they are introducing more and more new and improved types of resilient flooring that are durable, inexpensive, and easy for the amateur to install. In addition to these practical features, an equal amount of attention has been directed to offering designs and colors that will enhance any decorating scheme. Now you don't have to select flooring that will "go with everything" just because it's "safe." Select from wood-grain, parquet, marble, brick, cobblestone, terrazzo, and floral patterns in a wide range of decorator colors. As the patterns have become more glamorous, this type of flooring has been introduced into the kitchen, bathroom, utility room; in fact, into every room in the home.

Resilient floor coverings include inlaid linoleum, vinyl, rubber, vinyl asbestos, asphalt, and cork. These products come in 9- and 12-inch tiles; and 6-, 9-, and 12-foot width flooring.

When you are shopping for resilient flooring, don't let your choice be influenced entirely by color and pattern. Inquire about the characteristics of each type of material so you can choose the one that best fits your individual needs.

There are both tiles and sheet flooring that are simple for the do-it-yourselfer to install, if the floor underneath is sound. The paper-covered, adhesive-backed tiles are especially easy to install. Simply peel off the backing and press each tile into place. Although handling sheet flooring may seem more of a task, its lack of seams is an advantage. There are no cracks where dirt and dust can collect, or where moisture can seep through. In fact, some sheet flooring can be cut to fit with scissors, and simply laid in place without using any adhesive to hold them.

Unless subjected to unusual amounts of wear, resilient flooring requires thorough scrubbing or "wax stripping" only once or twice a year.

A cushioned vinyl flooring that combines the patterned appearance of carpet with the easy maintenance of vinyl is quite simple for the home handyman to install. Although it is ideal for kitchens, vinyl flooring is equally suited for any above-grade room in the home. The 12-foot widths mean seamless installation. Just cut to fit, and lay in place; no adhesive is necessary. Because of its high-density backing, it provides unexpected resiliency. It is soft underfoot, muffles noise, and reduces breakage of objects dropped on the floor. Its no-wax surface is impervious to normal household stains, and it retails for about $8 per square yard at flooring dealers.

If you have an entrance hall that gets lots of traffic, and the carpet shows every dirty footprint during the slushy months, don't be discouraged. Change to vinyl tile that is more practical and durable with very little expense and only a few hours of labor.

Here's how the entrance hall appeared after the vinyl tile installation had taken place. It took only two square yards of material, plus three hours of work to define the entrance area and reduce the maintenance chores to the bare minimum.

1. Remove quarter-round molding from around carpet edge, then cut away desired area of carpet and padding. Make certain that floor underneath is clean and free of wax. Cut felt paper to fit area and cement to floor. Let set for 24 hours before laying tiles. *2.* If you want to create a special design effect, work out the design with tiles placed on felt paper, and mark guidelines by snapping a piece of chalked string. Here, chalk lines indicate where narrow feature strips would be placed before adhesive was applied to permanently bond the tiles to the floor.

3. Carefully apply the adhesive to the felt paper only on the area that is to be immediately tiled. Spread the adhesive just to the chalk line, then position tile in line with the chalk mark. Press the tile in place, and proceed with the next area. *4.* Fold and tack carpet over edge of tiled entrance area. A metal carpet binder bar may be used to edge carpet, but there's a well-decorated look about the clean line of smooth tile contrasted against the textured carpet. Waxing of vinyl tile is optional since it has an exceptionally smooth, long-wearing surface.

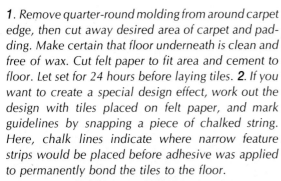

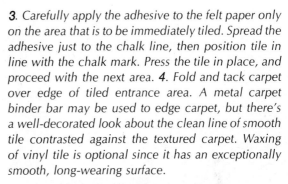

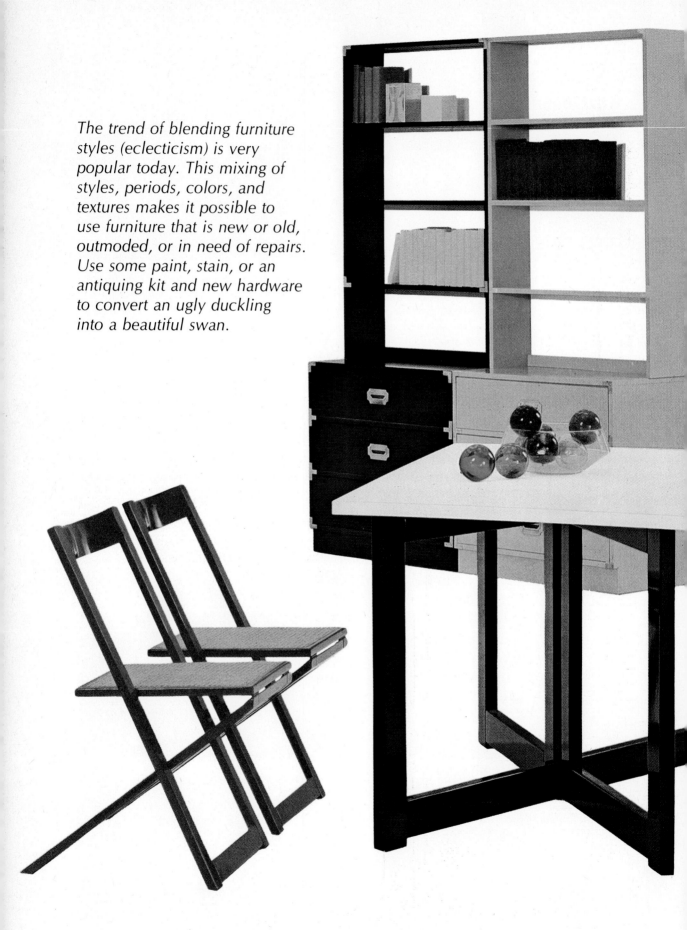

The trend of blending furniture styles (eclecticism) is very popular today. This mixing of styles, periods, colors, and textures makes it possible to use furniture that is new or old, outmoded, or in need of repairs. Use some paint, stain, or an antiquing kit and new hardware to convert an ugly duckling into a beautiful swan.

FURNITURE

Acquiring furniture for less than $100 is a challenge, but this task, hard as it may seem, is by no means impossible. It can be fun, exciting, and rewarding to see what you can accomplish by using your ingenuity. If you're willing to spend some time and effort, plus a small amount of money, you can change an ordinary room into something special — one that has a stamp of individuality.

Start with the furniture you have on hand, either those pieces you are presently using, or items that have been banished to the basement or attic. Next, turn to your family or friends for any castoffs that they might have accumulated. Look in secondhand stores, antique and thrift shops, at auctions, in classified columns, and on bulletin boards in offices and supermarkets.

Your only guidelines for selection (other than price) are the following: can the piece be useful as well as decorative, and does its condition merit the time and money you'll need to spend on it?

There are many ways to give a piece of furniture new life. One of the easiest ways is to paint it. You can also cover the piece with fabric or self-adhesive paper. Ornate, carved pieces, on the other hand, respond beautifully to antiquing and the new wood-grain finishes.

Quality woods such as walnut, cherry, and pine should be refinished with painstaking care in order to restore the warmth and beauty they originally had.

Trims and hardware can be added or removed to completely alter the character of any piece. Pulls, knobs, and wood trims are available in designs that range from contemporary to traditional.

New furniture needn't be taboo for your budget, either. Many wicker, wrought iron, metal and glass, molded plastics, and unfinished pieces are decorative and inexpensive.

Even if your budget is limited, your imagination need not be. You'll find suggestions on the following pages that will help you realize your furniture goals.

UPDATING YOUR FURNITURE

Very often, you can transform a humdrum room with ordinary furnishings into a beautiful one without casting out all the furnishings you already have. Possibly, you can achieve this by updating some of the furniture you have.

Take a good, close look at those items of furniture that show signs of wear, those that are hopelessly out-of-date, and those that have no distinctive design. These are often the best pieces for you to restyle and to update.

Look for upholstered pieces with simple lines and good-quality construction details. These can always be slipcovered, or reupholstered. If you have a fine piece that looks worn, say a Lawson sofa with straight lines, or a traditional wing-backed chair, cover it with a new fabric in a different color, pattern, or texture.

A tall chest, which gives a poorly proportioned appearance because its bulk rests on spindly legs, can take on grace and beauty if the legs are replaced with substantial ones that are in scale with the size of the chest. If your room is low-ceilinged, you may decide to lower the height of the chest by resting it on the floor, and not having any legs at all underneath it.

Tables can be updated without a great deal of work, or a lot of expense. Legs can be cut down if you want to lower them to coffee table height. They can be refinished, painted, or antiqued. If the tops are badly scarred, they can be covered with a new plastic laminate top.

Dining room furniture can be painted, refinished, or antiqued, and the fabric covering on the chair seats replaced. Use the same fabric for both draperies and the chair seats; and also to line the back of the china cabinet.

If it is at all possible, attempt these ideas before you dash out of the house to invest your money in new furniture pieces. You may be pleasantly surprised at the results you achieve.

You can convert an ordinary, outmoded piece of furniture into one that is attractive and useful if you preserve the good design elements and get rid of the undesirable features. The small chest, below at the left, was remodeled by removing the small door in the center and the flanking panels; the entire drawer was thrown away, and the top was ripped off. Then, the old varnish was removed with paint remover, taking care to get absolutely all the old finish off so that the stain, applied later, would go on evenly.

The original door was rehung, but placed over to one side. New panels were placed in the former drawer opening, and the remaining front opening. The new panels were inset from the divider strips so they would match the door and side panels. The new top was made with an opening for a copper "sink."

Stain that matched the old wood to the new wood was made from raw umber and raw sienna, linseed oil, and turpentine. After a coat of stain was applied overall, raw umber right from the tube was rubbed into all the corners and cracks to simulate an authentic antique finish. For a final professional touch, two coats of satin varnish were added. A copper sink was set in the opening for use as a planter, and a white china knob was attached to the door of the chest.

Restyling and refinishing furniture can be an absorbing leisure-time project and, when you think of the money you are saving, the job becomes even more satisfying. By investing only a small amount of money, plus your time, you can produce a handsome piece of furniture from one that is outmoded, and about to be discarded. You'll be surprised to see what you can do.

One of the most important aspects in restyling furniture is to be able to recognize which pieces are worthy of restyling. Make sure that they are structurally sound, or that the weak parts can easily be reinforced; and that there are good design elements that can be preserved. If you're a novice at this type of project, pick a simple piece of furniture to start with.

Decide first just where you will use the furniture. If it's going to take its place in a child's room or bedroom, no doubt you will take a different approach than if it will be used in a living room or entrance hall. Next, figure out what type of treatment will improve the piece, and how you will go about accomplishing it. If it's just a matter of painting or refinishing, or replacing old hardware with a newer version, the task is relatively simple. If it's necessary to change the basic structure in order to alter the appearance completely, the job will require some knowledge of carpentry.

Once you've decided to embark on a restyling and refinishing project, visit your building supply and paint dealer to find out what materials are available. New products that make it possible to do these jobs easier, quicker, and less expensively than ever before are appearing almost daily. In addition to paints, wood finishes, and antiquing kits, there are sculptured moldings, motifs, and panels that add elegance to furniture pieces. Also available are drawer pulls and knobs in wood, china, and metal finishes.

The table above at the left is one of the hexagon-shaped, too-high occasional tables that was common years ago. It's not old enough to be an antique, nor is it constructed of fine wood that should retain its natural finish. However, it's a type of table that can be turned into a good-looking furniture piece.

First, the bun feet were sawed off, and the knobby sections of the legs were cut off to lower the table height. After it was reassembled, the entire table was washed with liquid sander and treated to two coats of flat black enamel. Then, a coat of gray glaze was applied with a "dry brush" technique. The brush had been dipped into the paint and wiped almost dry, then lightly stroked over the table to bring out the highlights. Start with the brush practically dry, adding more until you get the right look.

A piece of black plastic laminate, cut to size, makes a practical, satiny-smooth tabletop. Apply contact cement to the plastic top, and to the old tabletop. Slip a sheet of brown wrapping paper between the top and the table to keep it from bonding while you position the laminate and the tabletop so they are exactly aligned. Tack chair leg glides to the bottom end of the legs, and you have a coffee table that will harmonize with any style of furnishings.

The office desk, chair, and metal filing cabinet shown on the opposite page are all sturdy and well made old-time pieces of discarded office furniture. They were purchased at bargain prices from a company that was redecorating and refurnishing its offices, and replacing outmoded equipment. All three pieces cost a lot less than it would have cost to purchase the wood to build the desk alone. Add to this a few dollars for refinishing materials, and a few hours of your spare time — space the working hours out over several evenings — and you will have a custom-tailored home office that is handsome, and functional.

1. The original molding around the top of a used desk, or almost any piece of old furniture that has had a lot of use, is usually too battered and scarred to be salvaged. Here, the old, damaged molding was pried off with a hammer and an old wood chisel.

2. The former molding was replaced with a piece of pine board cut the same thickness as the desk top. In order to attach it securely, use both glue and nails for application. Then, finish off the molding edge by applying walnut-finish edging tape to the molding with contact cement.

3. Next, remove all the old varnish down to the bare wood with a good-quality paint and varnish remover. After the wood has been thoroughly cleaned and sanded, you can apply a coat of dark walnut oil stain to make the wood appear darker, and more contemporary. Don't stain the desk top, as the contact cement requires an oil-free surface to adhere to.

4. Buy a sheet of plastic laminate, cut it exactly to fit out to the edge of the molding all the way around, and bond it to the old desk top with contact cement. Use a slip sheet of brown wrapping paper in between to aid in lining up the edges when the contact cement is ready to be permanently bonded.

5. Use a vinyl-coated upholstery fabric that matches the color of the desk top to cover the chair. As you remove the old upholstery fabric, pay careful attention to just how it was applied so that you can use the same method with the new material. Use the old material as a pattern to guide you in cutting the new fabric to just the right size. For a professional finish, trim with decorative upholstery nails.

6. To achieve the same wood-grain effect on the metal filing cabinet, as is on the desk, buy a refinishing kit in dark walnut. Apply the base coat first. Wipe on the stain, then brush in the grain lines, and rebrush across the grain. Add decorative, matching drawer pulls to both desk and filing cabinet. Use decorative wall hangings and table accessories, and floor length, openweave, textured draperies.

2

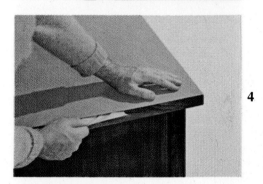

3

4

5

6

It isn't always necessary to strip the old finish off of a piece of furniture before you paint it. But, be sure to inspect it to see that there are no loose or wobbly pieces; if there are, mend them with furniture glue before you start the refinishing.

If the finish is sound—not blistered, cracked, or chipped—just wash it all over with liquid sander just before applying the base coat of paint. The chair above was treated to two coats of flat blue enamel. After the base coats, it was frosted with a white glaze—white enamel thinned to a waterlike consistency with turpentine. It was simply brushed on, then wiped off, leaving some in the grooves and around the spindles. If you'd rather, you can accomplish the same effect with an antiquing kit. You get the undercoat and glaze all in one package with complete instructions. Finish with two coats of dull varnish that will add a satin sheen and keep the glaze from wearing off or chipping easily.

Make patterns for the back and seat cushions from brown wrapping paper, allowing enough extra for seams. Make double welt seams. Pad the back with a piece of sponge rubber so that the back will hold its shape, and stuff the seat cushions with kapok. Use ties to hold the back cushion to the spindles.

1. Strip off old finish. If you plan to give furniture a natural, stained, or bleached finish, you must strip the old finish down to the bare wood first. Check for any loose joints, splits, or cracks in the wood and make all the repairs before you start to remove the old finish.

Brush paint and varnish remover generously over the entire surface, and wait until the finish becomes soft. Then, scrape the wood with a paint scraper. If there are crevices, curves, or carved parts that you can't reach with the scraper, use a fine-bristled wire brush or steel wool. If one coat isn't enough to remove all of the old finish, apply another coat of remover.

Next, clean off all the residue from the paint and varnish remover by rubbing the surface with #1 or #2 steel wool. Steel wool retains just the right amount of moisture for the wash-away type removers and, at the same time, provides the gentle abrasion that is needed. When all of the old finish is removed, rinse the piece with water, and wipe it with a clean, lint-free cloth.

Sandpaper, steel wool, and shaped sanding blocks are a big help in getting the wood clean and ready for the new finish. Start this step with coarse sandpaper; finish with a finer grade (at least 6/0), or wipe first with a liquid sander and then use a finer sandpaper. Be sure to sand with the grain of the wood, and not against it. After you are all through with the sanding, use a vacuum cleaner to get rid of as much sanding dust as possible. If you've done this stripping down part of the job well, you should be off to a smooth start for the finishing.

2. Applying varnish, lacquer, or stain. If your furniture is made of fine wood, you may want to emphasize the beauty of its grain and its natural color with only clear varnish or lacquer.

On the other hand, if you want to deepen the color of the wood and its grain pattern and contrast, start with a wiping stain. These wood stains are available in both wood colors and

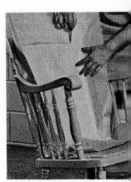

All the furniture pieces in the teen-age bedroom above were family cast-offs, or finds from secondhand furniture shops. The combination of the bright yellow, and the black and white houndstooth pattern creates a total effect that is lively and imaginative. The collection of wall hangings and accessories in the same colors helps achieve a youthful spirit.

nonwood shades. Read carefully and follow the manufacturer's directions that are printed on the label of the wood stain. Apply the stain with a soft, clean cloth, then wipe it off. The longer the stain remains on, the darker the wood will become. Feather and blend the edges so that they won't show. Stain waxes achieve the same effect, but be sure to select one that can be used under a good, highly wear-resistant topcoat.

A wood bleach can make even dark woods almost white, or any shade in between, without destroying the natural look. Brush the bleach on the bare wood according to the manufacturer's instructions, usually in two separate applications. Use an old, inexpensive brush. After bleaching, you can color with pigment stains which combine the natural attractiveness with hues not found in natural colors of woods.

3. Finishing the wood. Now, the wood is ready to receive the final finishing coats. The material you use depends on the amount of gloss desired.

Wood surfaces can now be made to look hand-rubbed with new semigloss and flat varnishes. Not only do you avoid long hours of rubbing, but the surface resists wear as well as most gloss varnishes on the market. These are intended as a topcoat only. You must use regular varnish or shellac first to build the finish properly.

For an open-pore finish where the wood pores remain clear and natural looking, skip the wood fillers and use only thin coats of varnish or other finishing material. Satin-finish brushing lacquer is an especially effective open-pore finishing material. Use it as a first coat, then finish with a synthetic-resin varnish.

Penetrating resin sealers, like those used for floors, are very reliable furniture finishes. They have extraordinary resistance to spotting,

If you can locate an old brass baby bed, you can convert it into a love seat like the one in the photo below. Seat and back cushions, and bolsters are covered with a paisley-patterned fabric, and accented with wall hangings, accessories, and pillows in pinks, yellows, and reds.

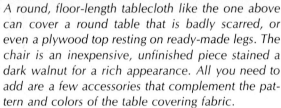

A round, floor-length tablecloth like the one above can cover a round table that is badly scarred, or even a plywood top resting on ready-made legs. The chair is an inexpensive, unfinished piece stained a dark walnut for a rich appearance. All you need to add are a few accessories that complement the pattern and colors of the table covering fabric.

Yellow is a happy color, and this combination bedroom, sitting room makes the most of it by accenting it with white and apple green. The floral pattern of the bedspread and covered cushions sets the color scheme, and the furniture pieces — none of them new — have been painted matching colors. All it takes to create a similar effect is imagination, paint, and fabric.

staining, marring, and scratching. The resin penetrates the wood and fills the pores; it becomes a finish in the wood rather than on the surface, yet the texture and the beauty of the wood is still clearly visible.

With any of these finishes, apply light coats, and sand between coats with fine steel wool. If you want a slightly higher gloss finish, and more protection from wear, give the finished surface a very thin coat of fine furniture wax.

If you have pieces of furniture that you want to enamel, prepare the wood in the same manner as you would for any other type of finish. Brush on two thin coats of a good-quality semigloss enamel in the color of your choice. After the first coat has dried, sand with fine steel wool. If you want to have a very high-gloss appearance, add a final coat of clear lacquer.

4. Antiquing. One of the most popular methods of refinishing furniture these days is with "antiquing kits." This is quick and easy to do, and the results are very effective. There is no limit to the style, size, or type of outdated furniture that you can refinish with these materials. You don't even have to remove the old finish first, unless it is badly chipped or cracked. Just wipe on a coat of liquid sander and sand down the rough spots. Next, apply one or two coats of undercoat paint. After the paint is thoroughly dry, paint on the glazing liquid. Finally, wipe the glazing liquid with a piece of cheesecloth until you achieve the exact effect you want.

All the materials, except the liquid sander, are included in the kit. There is a wide choice of colors that range from delicate pastels to beautiful simulations of real wood grains.

There are also many special effects that are easy to create with the antiquing materials.

A tortoiseshell pattern can be made by putting on a heavier than usual coat of glaze, and then simply tapping lightly with the tips of your spread fingers. Change the angle of your hand on each tap for a more random effect.

A splattern effect works only on horizontal surfaces. Dip a small, stiff brush in plain mineral spirits, then shake it out. Finish by thumbstroking spirits on newly glazed surface.

A stippled finish comes from jabbing a stiff, short-bristled paintbrush straight down—lightly —into the wet glaze. Work from the center out, and rotate the brush between the strokes for a random pattern effect.

A distressed wood appearance is achieved by making random scratches with the point of a nail, and dents with pieces of walnut shell or crushed rock pounded into the surface. Sand lightly, then rub raw umber artist's color into the dents, scratches, and edges. Rub off vigorously, leaving it darker around the edges.

Marbleizing starts with flat black enamel as an undercoat. When it is dry, paint on white glazing liquid or just flat white enamel thinned half and half with turpentine. Lay crumpled up pieces of plastic drop cloth—several feet square and somewhat flattened out—on top of the wet glaze. Pick up the pieces carefully without dragging them across the surface to give the marbleized effect. You can add more texture with a "splattern" effect of mineral spirits. Let it dry, and spray on two coats of clear finish.

A crumpled texture is made by crumpling up paper toweling, terry cloth, or tissue paper, and then jabbing it straight down into the glaze in a random, overlapping pattern.

A splatter pattern is put on over other patterns to add more interest and character. Do it the same as you would the splattern technique, but with the toothbrush dipped in glaze.

The snack table below was made from one pedestal-type leg removed from an old-fashioned library table, and topped with a 36-inch circle of ¾-inch plywood. The leg was refinished, and the top covered with ceramic tile and edged with stainless steel made to edge a kitchen counter. The leg and material cost $35.

You can rejuvenate any upholstered piece that's still usable, but looks drab. It takes about 11 yards of braid to transform a sofa by applying braid to sofa back, along edge of seat cushions, and on tailored skirt. Use fabric cement that is available in tubes at notions departments. The cost is around $11.

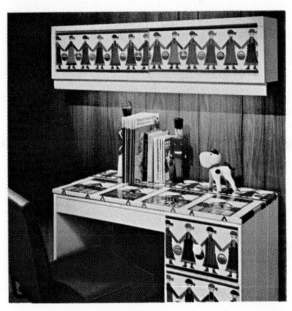

The unfinished desk and the wall-hung sliding-door cabinet above it have been glorified for a child's room. Both were covered with liquid laminate, then covered with colorful fabric, and topped with two more coats of the liquid. This is a quick and easy way to add a colorful surface that can withstand a lot of abuse. Fluorescent tube lighting has been mounted underneath the wall-hung cabinet, and a desk chair covered in durable vinyl-coated fabric.

The storage chest above has been given a custom look that makes it handsome enough for a living room or foyer. The unfinished chest was covered with 54-inch wide, richly textured vinyl fabric. Holes were drilled in the drawer fronts, and handles were formed with ⅝-inch manila rope. The rope ends were pulled through to the inside, splayed, and fastened securely with glue. The fabric color reappears in furniture pieces and accessories elsewhere in the room.

A distressed painted finish can be accomplished without a kit, and in a hurry, too. Use two contrasting colors of quick-drying spray-can enamels. Spray first with one color, and let it dry. Then lightly spray on the second color. When it dries, sand through the top coat into the underneath coat with #80 coarse sandpaper.

If you have furniture upholstered in plastic or vinyl leatherlike fabrics, or ottomans or cushions covered in this type of fabric, you can paint them to give them a new look. There is paint that retains its flexibility, and gives a new surface as well as a new color. Follow the directions printed on the label to ensure long wear, and a professional look.

There are zippered replacement cushions for Danish-style, maple, and wrought iron furniture that make chairs, settees, and sofas look like new again. The vivid striped, patterned, and solid-colored fabrics are longwearing and treated for soil resistance.

Inexpensive rocker and chair pads add comfort to wood chairs like Boston rockers, captain's, and Hitchcock arm and desk chairs. The colorful, tufted covers with matching ties, filled with latex foam, are made of durable fabrics.

Many of the ready-made slipcovers that are being offered now are made of a stretch-type nylon-cotton blend fabric that allows them to mold to the shape of the furniture. They fit most of the popular styles of furniture and come in a variety of attractive colors and patterns.

Custom-made slipcovers are more expensive, but they offer a broader choice of fabrics, colors, and patterns. Also, the same fabric can be repeated in draperies, pillows, and table covers. If you want them professionally tailored, get several estimates, as labor costs vary. Also, ask to see examples of finished slipcovers, as there can be a great deal of difference in the quality of workmanship. If you can make them yourself, you can cut the cost to the bare minimum.

You can buy inexpensive, unfinished furniture in almost any style these days. It is usually made from rather inexpensive wood, however, and needs some special finishing touches to give it a custom look. The hutch above was painted white, the drawer front and sliding doors covered with walnut veneer, the stock grooved doors replaced with sliding doors made of 1/8-inch hardboard, and the wood knobs replaced with metal hardware.

BUYING FURNITURE UNDER $100

Most people change the paint, wall coverings, draperies, even some of the accessories, every five or six years, or oftener. But, when they are buying furniture they expect to live with it for many years. In order to find furniture pieces priced under $100 that feature good design and sturdy construction details, it does take some searching. However, it's worth the effort, and the results are surprising. The selection of furniture in the economy price range is much greater than most people think.

It isn't always necessary to purchase expensive dining room chairs to create an attractive, comfortable room setting. You can find director's chairs in painted or natural wood finishes with canvas backs and seats that can be purchased for about $18 each. The same style, with metal frames and vinyl upholstery fabric, is well suited to contemporary furnishings, and sells for about $30. Another good feature—they can be folded and stored in a small area. When the time comes that you can replace them with chairs of fine furniture wood, you can always move them to the family room or a bedroom.

This is the same hutch that appears on the opposite page. To duplicate this finishing treatment, cover the drawer front and the sliding doors, which have replaced the stock grooved doors, with thin sheets of walnut veneer. Finish the walnut veneer the same as you would finish solid walnut. Sand it first, then use a sealer, and lastly finish it with a coat of varnish or wax. Veneer is available at most lumberyards.

White semigloss enamel sets off the areas of walnut. To prepare the wood for enamel coats, fill all dents and nail holes with water-base putty, and sand when dry. Then, apply a coat of pigmented resin sealer. Sand with 220 grit sandpaper, and dust all surfaces before applying enamel. Apply two coats of enamel, brushing it out well. Be sure to sand and dust well between the two coats of enamel, too.

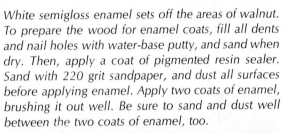

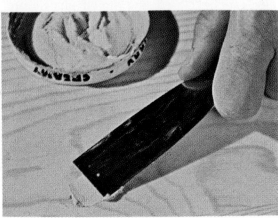

The corner shelf unit and table in the entrance hall above are inexpensive and simple to assemble. Both are made of hardwood turnings that can be purchased at lumberyards. Simply twist spindles together with threaded dowels. The prices of the items, unfinished, are about $48 for the table in classic style, and about $40 for the traditional corner unit.

Your bathroom will take on a new, high-fashion roominess with the addition of an elegant long-lined etagere like the one above. Five shelves provide extra space for linens and grooming accessories. Available in brass plate with white glass shelves or Danish nickel with black glass shelves, it sells for about $75. The 60-inch high etagere has 12-inch square shelves.

The same applies to a comfortable lounge chair for the living room. You can buy a bentwood rocker with a cane back and seat for about $80 that will be at home with any style of furnishings. You may become so attached to it that you will decide to keep it, even after you add a large, expensive upholstered chair.

For the young at heart, there are inflatable chairs, love seats, sofas, and ottomans made of treated, heavy-duty vinyl. They also come in small sizes for children. Priced from $8 to $30, they come in vivid blue, red, yellow, white, and black colors, and in jungle stripes. For the mobile society, this furniture can simply be deflated when moving day rolls around, then pumped up again when put in new surroundings.

There are glass-topped tables in many sizes, shapes, and heights. Some have shiny metal legs, and some have tops that rest on a wood base with a gold leaf finish. Their see-through look adds sparkle to a room without appearing to take up space. Many of these are priced well under $100.

If you need extra seating for family dinners, card games, meetings, television, and parties, there are stackable folding chairs available that closely resemble dining chairs of fine wood in traditional or modern designs. They have hardwood frames in a walnut finish, vinyl-covered foam-padded seats; some even have cane inserts in the backs. They are simple to set up, and they can be closed and stored quickly and compactly. They sell for $15 to $20 each.

There is a whole, wide, wonderful world of wicker furniture, and it is all reasonably priced. No longer is wicker furniture confined to porches, patios, and sunrooms. It can be used in any room, indoors or outdoors, in its natural color, or spray-painted whatever color you choose. There are chairs, sofas, stools, chests, headboards, desks, nightstands, folding screens, and hampers in prices that range from $10 to $100. Many pieces are all wicker; some tables and chairs have wrought iron legs. Also available are contemporary and oriental designs, and the

Victorian-styled pieces that were popular many years ago. The Victorian pieces are just as fashionable today. One or more pieces of wicker furniture can fit into any room, and complement any style of furnishings. There are also chairs with wood frames and woven backs and seats; seats without legs that hang from the ceiling.

You can find Parson's tables in high gloss lacquer finishes—black, white, green, blue, red, and yellow—in several sizes and heights for less than $100. The same table design in wormy chestnut, measuring 18 inches square and 18 inches high, retails for approximately $65.

Ready-to-finish furniture is the low-cost answer to many decorating-on-a-budget problems.

In addition to the usual traditional, contemporary, or early American offerings that have been around for years, there are now unfinished Parson's tables in at least five sizes that sell for $15 to $30; and complete groupings of campaign furniture accented with brass-plated antiqued drawer pulls and side handles priced from $25 on up. Both of these designs have a practical, rugged style that makes them exciting furniture pieces. They are especially suited to a high gloss enamel finish that resembles lacquer, but they can also be done in a wood tone.

These are all suggestions for buying new furniture. There's also the other-than-new pieces you can find at resale shops or house sales.

If you happen to find a glass-doored cabinet that resembles the one that is pictured at the right, give it an antique finish, and line it with mirrors; you will have a handsome and useful piece of furniture. This corner cabinet, which was a secondhand store find, responded very well to the mirror-lining treatment. You can use custom-cut mirrors, and mount them; or use two or three mirrors that fit the length of the inside of the back of the cabinet.

Choosing airy rattan chairs with colorful cushions that add comfort, such as the two pictured below, offers an inexpensive solution to a decorating problem. Part of their charm lies in the fact that they are equally at home for either indoor or outdoor living, and are compatible with any style of furnishings. You can purchase chairs of this design for approximately $17.50 each without the cushions; with the cushions, they sell for about $27 each.

BUILDING FURNITURE

Be optimistic in your approach to building furniture. Even though it may sound like a job for only a skilled cabinetmaker, actually there are many items that can be built successfully by the home handyman. There are so many new and improved materials to work with—wood veneers and plastic laminates in sheet form, wood finishes and enamels—that it is possible to give a fine furniture appearance to pieces constructed of inexpensive lumber. If you don't have the tools for the furniture project you are planning, don't think that you have to go out and buy them—you can always rent them at reasonable rates.

It is much easier to achieve professional results if you choose to make furniture pieces of simple design—those which feature straight lines and rectangular shapes. It is more satisfying to build a simple item because you're more likely to achieve a professional handcrafted look. You can always attempt something more complicated as you become more skilled in woodworking.

Take a good look at each room in your home; then decide just what you need to add to existing furniture to make your home more livable. Plan your project carefully—take accurate measurements to eliminate wasting materials. Choose a style and a size that is compatible with the furniture you already have.

You can add a dining area in your kitchen by building a single-leg breakfast table like the one below. Design the shape of the top to fit the space you have. Cut it out of doubled ¾-inch plywood. Cover and edge table with plastic laminate. Buy leg and drawer units at a building supply company. Mount a 1 x 8 pine shelf on the wall above the table. The cost: about $60.

You can build this rugged desk for a teen-ager's room from rough six-inch planks, edged with three-inch boards. Sand only the roughest edges. Finish the desk with a commercial combination stain and sealer. A pair of cross legs nailed together supports the sturdy desk top. Another budget idea is the director's chair, in black for an expensive look. Cost: about $50.

You can easily make this four-foot long coffee table. First, cut ¾-inch plywood for the top, then fasten 18-inch legs to the top, and add the 1 x 2 stretchers. Use walnut for both the legs and stretchers. Apply a sheet of laminated plastic to the top and trim the edges. Finish the edges by cementing on a walnut edging tape. The materials cost about $25.

The coffee table and end table below are so simple to make that an amateur can tackle them. The tabletop was rescued from an old dresser, and refinished. The end table and coffee table base are sheets of three-inch thick cork purchased from a cork supplier. They were cut into 18-inch squares and stacked up. You can build both of these items for about $7.

This easy-to-make half-table is 15 inches deep, and is fastened to the wall with brackets at 30 inches from the floor. Two 2 x 4s are used for front legs. This shelf-table, painted to match furnishings, serves as both a lamp table and a bookcase; with the ottoman pulled into place, it can serve as either a dressing table or a desk. The cost is about $65.

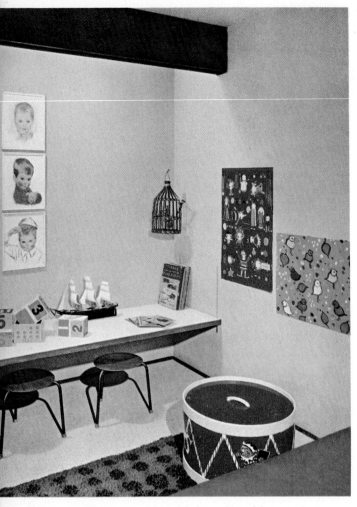

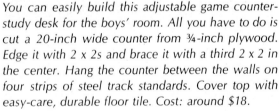

You can easily build this adjustable game counter-study desk for the boys' room. All you have to do is cut a 20-inch wide counter from ¾-inch plywood. Edge it with 2 x 2s and brace it with a third 2 x 2 in the center. Hang the counter between the walls on four strips of steel track standards. Cover top with easy-care, durable floor tile. Cost: around $18.

For about $10 you can build this 24-inch cube table with concealed storage. Made of ½-inch plywood, it has a hinged front that houses a record player and amplifier. To duplicate the montage effect, clip magazine photos and glue them to the top and sides of cube. Let dry, then apply several coats of clear-plastic sealer. Top with a high-gloss finish.

You may need tables. If so, consider the cube-type and its infinite decorative potential. First, construct an ordinary 18 x 18-inch square cube of ¾-inch plywood. Then, decide what finish will be the most suitable for your room.

To go with Mediterranean furnishings, you could cover the cube with vinyl floor covering in a Spanish design. All you need is a one-yard remnant of a six-foot wide floor covering. Cut five 18-inch square pieces and apply them to the

sides and top of the cube with adhesive. The cost of the table will depend on whether you get a good bargain on the remnant, but it shouldn't be more than about $20 in all. If you have country-style furnishings, you can use the same method, but choose a brick or stone pattern.

For a contemporary look, cover the cube with shiny, stainless tiles. This will cost about $28. Or you can use sheets of miniscule mirrors and apply them with special mirror mastic. Finish off the top edge with a stainless steel rim. Miter the corners, and attach it with epoxy. Cost: about $44. Iron-on plastic laminate in a wood-grain finish also has a modern look; this will cost about $36 for a handsome cube table.

For the chess players in the family, cover the sides of the cube with alternating black and white vinyl floor tile. For the top, cut the black and white tiles into two-inch squares (use a jig saw for uniformity) to form a chess board design. Apply the squares to the cube with floor tile adhesive. Cost: about $20.

You may want to build a piece of furniture to show off your favorite accessories. If so, why not build a rugged centipede table that gets its name from its many legs? For the top, cut eight-foot lengths of a 2 x 4, a 2 x 6, and a 2 x 8. You will need 38 legs for this size. Join the planks together with a 2 x 4 at each end on the top and fasten with machine bolts at both ends of the three planks. Rest the top on a ¼-inch plywood base. Make the legs of the fiber inside rollers from bolts of fabric and carpeting in 1¾-inch, 2¼-inch, and 2½-inch diameter sizes. Cut the tubes in 9-inch lengths, and glue them to the base in pairs with epoxy. Paint the finished table in a color that harmonizes with your color scheme, and the legs in a darker color for contrast. The cost is only about $20. Place the table against the wall, arrange accessories on it, and hang a large wall hanging above it.

You can build a simple four-foot long coffee table for about $25. First, cut the top of ¾-inch plywood, fasten 18-inch legs to it, and add stretchers of 1 x 2s. Then, apply a laminated plastic top and trim the edges. Use walnut for the legs and stretchers, and cement on a walnut edging strip around the laminated plastic top.

These are only a few suggestions that may inspire you to build furniture pieces you need.

The wall-hung dressing table below offers a perfect solution for a bedroom or dressing room that lacks the space for freestanding furniture. The shelf can easily be made from a discarded table or dresser top. Paint it to harmonize with the furnishings in the room, and attach it to the wall with ornamental shelf brackets in a painted or metallic finish. Mount a large hanging mirror above the shelf, and place a lamp for convenience. Add a swivel-type piano stool that has been refinished and recushioned.

It is not a difficult project to build a two-legged table like the one below, and attach it to the wall. For floor covering, add vinyl asbestos tile, alternating squares of two colors, and use mastic to install it. Paint walls, table, and chairs a vivid shade of your favorite color. Make chair cushions of bold-patterned fabric, treated for soil resistance, and use the scraps to make mats for wall hangings. Add place mats and tableware in bright colors, and you have a dining area that is bright and cheerful.

Building outdoor furniture that will meet the needs of your family requires only a small investment of time and money, but the rewards are many. Outdoor living is a popular family activity, and it is available to everyone. It isn't limited to those who have a large home with acres of lawn, a patio, and a pool. Even if you have only a mini-backyard, or an apartment with a balcony, you can build outdoor furniture that will add to the pleasures of carefree outdoor activities—dining, recreation, or just loafing.

There is nothing more delightful for your patio or sundeck than a small pool. You can build a pool-and-bench combination with a low surface that is ideal for sitting or serving, in addition to adding the cool beauty of a serene bit of water. This is really a simple project. Just build a large plywood box, and line it with fiber glass for waterproofing; put a plug in the bottom for easy draining. Fasten a plywood bench all around the top; paint it with exterior paint, or stain it in a wood finish or finish it with a coat of weather-resistant sealer. If you add lights underneath the bench, they will add nighttime glamour. This pool-and-bench combination costs about $40 to build. (To obtain this plan, order Project Plan 3506-2 from Reader Service, 1A5, 1716 Locust St., Des Moines, Iowa 50336.)

You can build a barbecue cart on wheels to hold your portable charcoal grill, and all the gear that goes with it. The cabinet under the grill can be used to store charcoal, hickory chips, and other necessities. When the top sections are open, and the front folded down, you can use these surfaces for cooking and serving. When you are through with the meal, simply close up the barbecue cart and roll it out of the way. This project only costs about $25 for materials, and you can get the plans for it. (To obtain Project Plan 3506-3, write Reader Service, 1A5, 1716 Locust St., Des Moines, Iowa 50336.)

Why not build a patio bench that also has the added advantage of storage facilities? You'll have no trouble building a bench of plywood with a few 2 x 4s for bracing and legs. It's no more complicated than building a simple box. You just glue and nail the panels together. Attach the top with hinges, so you can keep garden tools, cushions, and other outdoor equipment right on the patio where it is always handy. Paint it with waterproof enamel. This bench will only cost about $16 for materials.

For complete relaxation, many people prefer a hammock. You can make one out of three yards of 36-inch wide canvas and small amounts of colorful fabric for applique patterns. Cut the

You can put together this sturdy slat bench in just a few hours, and add a decorative and useful accent to your patio at the same time. The bench is made of redwood 2 x 4s with short lengths of 1 x 2s sandwiched between them. After you have cut all the pieces, simply nail the first 2 x 4 frame together, using waterproof glue at the mitered joints. Use this frame as a pattern for all the rest; then glue and nail in the blocks. Cost: about $14.

This wrap-around planter-bench can be built for about $20 (not including plants). First, build a hexagonal planter box of 2 x 6-inch fir boards, each side 30 inches across. Paint surfaces exposed to soil with wood preservative. Use 2 x 4s for frames and legs of the three benches. Nail legs to inside of planter, and toenail boards between rear legs to hold soil away from base of tree trunk. Cut redwood 2 x 4s for bench tops and nail to frame.

The serviceable cover-up for the barbecue below was built for about $41. Walls are firebricks—seven lengths long and four wide—with draft hole and gravel-covered firebox. Top of resawn redwood (with 2 x 4 frame) fits over barbecue after it has cooled, and serves as a table, seat, or spot for sunbathing.

You can have a conversation piece-patio table for about $58 when you mix pioneer artifacts with twentieth-century plastic. Take a vintage stoneware pickling crock and top it with an old wagon wheel. Cover the wheel with ¼-inch thick plastic, cut to fit over the rim and around the hub, so it won't slide.

These outdoor pedestal tables cost only about $7.50 each. Bases are constructed of drainage or flue tiles; tops, of steppingstones. Dig a hole and sink a tile, flange end up. Fill with sand. Use latex patching to fill the last inch or two, and as adhesive around the edge. Choose steppingstones about 18 inches in diameter—set in place; let concrete patching cure.

fabric into large, bold designs, and applique onto the canvas. Hem the canvas at both ends and space out metal eyelets along both hemmed edges. Use nylon cord to thread the eyelets to the tubular, metal frame. Cost: about $17.50.

For only about $17.50, you can build a patio table with storage underneath for cushions. The three-foot square top is made of quarry tile that can be exposed to all kinds of weather. Use ¾-inch plywood for the top, and attach the six-inch square tiles with mastic. Seal the surface with grout between the tiles. Place the top on two-inch square legs that are set 18 inches apart, and are 18 inches high. Build a plywood shelf to form a low brace between the legs, and use this to store the chair and bench cushions when they are not in use.

You can build a sturdy bench that will be a welcome addition to any patio when it is placed against a privacy screen, or wall. You will need four pairs of 1 x 3-inch steel legs welded to a steel cross brace. Use this frame to support four 18-foot long 4 x 6s that form a 15-inch high seat. Set the bottoms of the legs in concrete. Cover six 24-inch square cushions with canvas in different bright colors, and attach them with canvas snaps to the 2 x 4-inch runners nailed to the wall behind the bench. Materials cost about $98.

As you survey your own needs, you may decide you want to alter or adapt these designs to better fit your style of living. These are just a few suggestions regarding various types of outdoor furniture that are easy-to-build, easy on the budget, decorative, and useful.

Patio tables, one lighted, are made from precast concrete blocks. Use blocks with patterned perforations for legs, and top with cap blocks. Paint concrete if you wish. Put a light inside unit; plug extension cord into grounded electrical outlet. Lighted table is 15 inches high; the other is 18. Cost: about $15.50.

Here's a picnic table with attached benches that you can build yourself for about $15. Use 2 x 2 redwood slats to form the table and bench tops, and frame them with 2 x 4s. Brace the table from below with bench supports attached to the backs of vertical supports that repeat the parquet motif of the top.

You can build these piggyback benches for about $22. Use 2 x 2s to form legs, braces, and runners. Legs of big bench are 15 inches tall, small ones are 9 inches. Screw inside-corner braces between legs, runners, and cross braces. Prefabricated deck planks form the bench tops.

Use decorative screens and room dividers to organize and divide limited space to accommodate your family's multipurpose and diverse activities.

SCREENS & DIVIDERS

Screens and dividers play an important role in home decorating today. In fact, they have become an established architectural concept. They offer the advantage of a partition without the expense of structural alterations. And their mobility makes it possible to position and reposition them according to family needs.

These movable walls not only add decorative interest to rooms, they also help define areas without restricting their usefulness to a single purpose. In small homes, or apartments, you can even create an illusion of separate work, play, study, hobby, and conversation areas where none existed before. There are literally dozens of practical and functional room arrangements and re-arrangements that are possible with screens and dividers.

You can create a separate entryway or hallway, divide the living room from the dining area, divide the breakfast area from the work end of the kitchen, and break up awkward lengths of wall space.

Large or small they create havens of privacy that keep childish chaos from intruding on adult order. They can also help to keep family noise from distracting one member's need for a quiet place to study.

Ready-made offerings come in a wide variety of materials—wood, metal, plastic, glass, plexiglass, pierced masonry, perforated hardboard, veneers woven into panels of open and closed designs, hardwood spindles, see-through shelves.

Dividers can be freestanding, supported by suspension-type poles, or permanently attached to a framework that is fastened to the ceiling and the floor. Dividers made of fabric can hang from regular traverse rods.

If you want to make your own screens or dividers, use any of the above-mentioned materials, plus hardboard covered with fabric, wallpaper, or adhesive-backed vinyl. Put your imagination to work, you can design and make a screen or divider that is both decorative and functional with only a small investment.

This easy-to-assemble space divider requires no installation, as it is supported by square, metal tension poles. Panels shown here in Venetian gold finish (also available in antique silver and black) closely resemble welded metal sculpture. Poles adjust from seven feet ten inches to eight feet four inches, and can be made taller with 12-inch extensions. The price is about $90 for the size shown above.

This room divider with crystal-clear panels, which reflect light, and sparkle in contrast to the square, modern poles finished in matte black, has spring-tension poles that adjust to ceiling height. The same model also comes in a shiny, all-white finish. You can find these dividers in furniture, department, and decorating specialty stores throughout the country. The size shown here retails for less than $80.

SCREENS AND DIVIDERS TO BUY

Homemakers throughout the country are becoming increasingly aware of the versatility, flexibility, and decorative possibilities of screens and room dividers. There are designs, colors, and materials to suit any style of furnishings, and sizes to fit any room. Screens come with three, four, five, or six hinged panels; most dividers come in sections that can be joined together to create as much separation as is desired. Both screens and dividers are available in many inexpensive versions. They are easy to install and easy to move as space requirements change.

Lightweight plastic panels with the beauty of stained glass come in decorator colors and are supported by wood frames that extend from floor to ceiling. These may be obtained at building supply stores. There are also folding screen panels with panels of the same plastic. You can even get panels of perforated hardboard in a variety of designs, panels of cane or woven veneer, or woven metal mesh for these frames.

Freestanding hardwood divider units that need no nuts or bolts to assemble are available in wood-tone or painted finishes. These are suitable for any room in the home and may consist of shelves only, or a combination of open shelves and storage units—glass or wood door cabinets, desks, or three-drawer chests, or lift-lid vanities. You can assemble as many units as are necessary to fill your individual needs. These can be purchased in home furnishings departments.

You can buy unfinished cubes, cabinets, and bookshelves in several sizes that are polished, sanded, and ready for painting or staining. All you have to do is stack them up in whatever arrangement pleases you, and you have a room divider combined with invaluable storage space.

There are twist-together hardwood spindles that you can buy in 15-inch lengths to create whatever size room divider fits your room requirements. These come unfinished and can be painted or finished with a wood-tone stain.

For those who want room dividers that can be moved easily, you can buy ones with spring-loaded suspension poles that hold panels firm between ceiling and floor. They need no brack-

ets and leave no holes. The panels are made of translucent polystyrene in bottle glass patterns, wrought iron panels in lacy, filigree designs, bamboo panels with an openwork pattern of stalks and leaves, woven reed with a basket-weave effect, and perforated hardboard.

Louvered shutters, in either painted or wood-tone finishes, can be bought in sizes suitable for either folding screens or room dividers.

Steel storage shelving with a tough baked-on beige or gray scratch-resistant enamel finish comes in many sizes. These freestanding units can be arranged to serve as dividers and provide extra storage space in family rooms, work shops, utility rooms, and children's rooms.

Folding screens with three, four, five or six plywood panels range in price from $12 to $30. Two-way hinges allow panels to fold forward or backward. These can be stained or painted, or covered with fabric or wall covering.

A single, tall shutter acts as a divider in the bathroom below. Trim the shutter to fit, cutting floor and ceiling moldings, if necessary. Toenail the shutter at the top and bottom, and add quarter-round moldings on both sides of the top and the bottom, and on the side where it joins the wall. Paint the shutter to match woodwork. This gives an illusion of a compartmented bathroom. Cost: about $21.50.

These portable patio screens cost only about $9 each. They are simply bamboo shades that provide privacy and protection against harsh sunlight, and let air filter through. You can easily remove them for storage, or for a more open look. Make frames of 2 x 2-inch redwood and install spring plungers at the tops to hold them against the ceiling. Secure matchstick bamboo shades to the frames with screen molding.

100

SCREENS AND DIVIDERS TO BUILD

You can be sure of having the design you want, plus the practical features you need if you make screens or dividers yourself. Whether you want simple folding screens, see-through walls, or freestanding units, the cost will be nominal if you provide the labor. Before you shop for materials, make up your mind just what style, design, color, and size will be most compatible with the style of furnishings you have. Measure your room and the ceiling height, and take these dimensions with you on your shopping tour.

You can build a beautiful burlap-covered screen in a few hours, for only about $10. Just make three frames of 1 x 2-inch wood strips. Staple on the burlap and join the panels with double-acting screen hinges. Make big splashy circle designs by cutting stencils from cardboard. Lay the screen flat and mask around the stencil with newspaper. Spray-paint four circles vertically on each panel, in several colors.

Another idea for a decorative screen is to start by building the panels from ¾-inch plywood. Cover the panels with vinyl-coated paper, felt, or other solid color fabric. You can attach

This five-panel, cotton fabric divider can be made for about $21. Cut two lengths for each panel; turn face to face and machine sew. Turn and press. Use harmonizing colors for rectangles, circles, and hand applique. Hang panels on a wood or brass rod suspended from ceiling by brass chains. Insert rod through panels, about 10 inches from the bottom.

The dead space around a stairwell comes alive in no time when surrounded with colorful plastic panels like those above. You can buy panels in the color and pattern of your choice at building supply stores. Use 1 x 2s for the frames; groove and stain them. You can add this treatment to a stairwell for about $75.

Cut the mosque-shaped opening for this divider in two matching pieces of ⅜-inch plywood; line the inside of the opening with sheet aluminum. Build the partition framework from 2 x 4s, and cover it with the ⅜-inch plywood pieces. Fasten a 1 x 4 to the wall with toggle bolts. Slide edges of plywood partition over this board and secure in place with nails. This bathroom divider can be built for less than $25.

You can build this divider in a child's room for about $16. Buy three, 4 x 4 fir posts. Drill holes for ¾-inch dowels at 6-inch intervals on alternate sides. Nail 4-foot 2 x 4s to the floor and ceiling; fit posts between them and toenail in place. Cut dowels to lengths of eight inches, apply glue, and tap them in place.

You can build this two-faced divider of plastic-coated perforated hardboard for about $64. Cut double sheets of hardboard; then to hold hardboard, rabbet studs or nail quarter round the length of the panels. Position and plumb panels between. Finally, mount brackets and plywood shelves covered with laminated plastic.

This screen panel divider covers the radiator and bookshelves in the living room below when it is closed, and swings open to provide a cover-up for the dining area beyond. Set the panels of filigree wood into a framework of hardwood strips. Hang with a continuous hinge. Divider can be built for about $82.

the covering either with glue, or by stapling. Join the panels with double-acting screen hinges. Now, add a border and design of decorative cloth tape. Use spray adhesive to apply the tape, then use more of the same tape on pillows and tablecloths for a coordinated look. This screen costs about $22 to build.

You can also cover the same type of screen with printed fabric that is also used for draperies or laminated window shades, and chair cushions. This gives the room a one-fabric look.

One of the simplest, most effective, and most colorful room dividers is made with ball fringe. String the fringe on fiber thread and attach it to strips of wood at the top and bottom.

An elegant space divider can be made from decorative drapery rods for about $62. Use five six-foot, white-and-gold wood drapery rods with matching four-inch finials. Suspend the rods on ⅝-inch wood dowels three feet long whose ends are inserted into floor-to-ceiling wood poles. Paint the side poles and dowels white. Insert lengths of wide ribbon in a contrasting color between each of the rods for a striped effect.

Why not make a freestanding divider from panels of ¼-inch hardboard, 16 inches wide and six feet long? Select tempered hardboard that is smooth on both sides. Cover the hardboard pan-

els with adhesive-backed vinyl in a realistic wood-tone pattern. Simply slip the panels into ready-made 1 x 2-inch hardboard stops, painted a flat or lacquered black. The stops, measuring five feet two inches long, extend one inch beyond the vinyl-covered hardboard. Glue and nail the panel to side rails made of 1 x 4-inch lumber.

You can build a portable room divider screen for a kitchen to separate the areas for eating and cooking for about $26. Use two spring-tension poles at the top to hold the divider steady. Frame the unit with 2 x 2 posts and 1 x 2 crosspieces; fill the spaces between with squares of ½-inch flakeboard and panes of colored glass.

If you want to divide the space in a bedroom occupied by two girls, place the chests of drawers back-to-back in the middle of the room and build a see-through wall of wood filigree above the chests. This gives an illusion of privacy.

You can even build a simple space divider out of 2 x 4s. Have lumber cut to size so it fits exactly from floor to ceiling. Cover each 2 x 4 with felt. Wedge divider posts solidly to the ceiling with gasket material so that if you want to move them there will not be a single nail hole or mark.

If you have a large living room, but no foyer, you can separate the entryway from the living room with a wall of pierced masonry.

You can suggest a division of space as shown in the bedroom below by building a partial see-through divider. Vertical 2 x 4 posts were fastened to a horizontal strip at floor and ceiling. Crossbars were then spaced at intervals between the verticals. The divider was painted a deep pink to complement the room's color scheme. The sleeping area has an area rug; the sitting room has a vinyl tile flooring.

If you want to semi-separate one area from the rest of the room, try this fabric divider treatment. Deep, scalloped valance and tieback draperies define the dining area at one end of this living room and minimize the slant of the ceiling. The valance hangs from 1 x 3s secured to the ceiling, while the draperies are installed in a track fastened to a 2 x 8 beam extending across the entire width of the room.

This outdoor center is easy to assemble, and to knock apart. Make four planters of red cedar 1 x 2s; saw notches half the width of each, three inches from the ends. No bottoms needed; just slip them together. Build redwood benches 18 inches high; then the 5½-foot cedar fence. Use 1 x 1s spaced on two-inch centers and nail to 1 x 4 stringers at top and bottom. No posts are required; simply nail easy-to-handle fence sections to benches and planters.

If you want to have privacy, and protection from harsh sunlight, you can build portable patio screens for about $9 each. Make frames of 2 x 2-inch redwood and install spring plungers at the tops to hold them secure against the ceiling. Fasten matchstick bamboo blinds to the frames with screen molding. These are easy to remove for storage or for a more open look.

An inexpensive way to add life and color to a divider is through the use of plants and foliage. If you have a see-through divider with either wood or glass shelves, arrange potted plants on the shelves, interspersed with crystal and colored glass, decorative accessories. If you have a wood-paneled divider or folding screen, group tall plants against it for extra emphasis.

Take advantage of the many possibilities that folding screens and room dividers offer for conquering your space problems. With the variety of styles available, and the wide range of materials on the market, you are bound to find one that will be perfect in your home.

It isn't always the amount of storage facilities that you have, but the way you organize them that makes the difference between order and confusion. Here's a collection of exciting storage ideas that are inexpensive, practical, and decorative. Follow the suggestions on the following pages, and you will be able to put things where they are readily accessible.

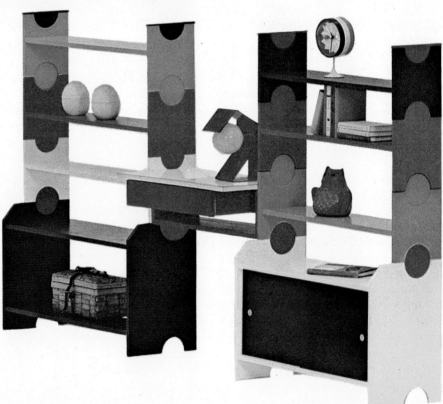

SHELVES & STORAGE

Today, there is a greater need for storage space than ever before. This is just as true in large homes as it is in small ones, or in apartments.

Families today have more clothing—for all seasons, all kinds of sports and recreational activities—than ever before. They have books, records, toys, collections, hobby materials, luggage, sports equipment, lawnmowers, and the once-a-year items such as Christmas and holiday decorations. And when you add to this conglomeration the large number of appliances, tools, and gadgets found in every household, it is no wonder most families need more storage space.

The following pages are devoted to a discussion of this very common problem. And believe it or not, there are many ways to solve the problem.

The first step in storage-space planning is to take an inventory of existing storage facilities. If you scrutinize these areas carefully, you will probably find that you aren't putting them to the best possible use. If closets and cupboards are cluttered with clothing and household items that are no longer in use, this is a good time to discard some of these items. Although you may think that every inch of storage space is in use, you can make many minor alterations that will add up to greater efficiency.

The next step is to take a good look to see if you have any storage pieces that can be updated. Many times, an about-to-be-discarded cabinet, chest of drawers, or dresser that seems hopelessly outmoded can be revitalized.

Next, check for storage pieces that you can buy or build. Wall units with shelves, or a combination of shelves and cupboards and/or a desk, can be either wall-hung or freestanding. In addition to chests, cabinets, and shelf units, manufacturers offer well-designed multi-purpose furniture pieces. Also available are inexpensive closet and cupboard organizers that will literally double existing storage facilities.

You can accomplish a cabinet rejuvenation like the one above for about $38. Use a wheat-type wallpaper paste to bond the fabric on the flush wood doors. Let it dry overnight. Glue and tack the finished ⅛-inch plywood panels over the fabric. Protect the fabric from soiling by spraying it with a coat of clear plastic that is available in paint departments. Finish it with two coats of semigloss enamel and a coat of glaze for an antique finish. Repeat the fabric that is used in the door panels in draperies at the kitchen windows. Add canisters, table linens, dishes, and decorative accessories in the same shades of purple, blue, and green for a coordinated effect.

UPDATING STORAGE SPACE

One of the easiest and least expensive ways to add storage or shelf space in your home is to convert or update one or more of the pieces of furniture that you have around the house.

If you've been a homemaker for a number of years and are still using at least some of the furniture you bought when you first set up housekeeping, this message is especially for you. You probably have one or more pieces that are so poorly designed or outmoded that you wonder what ever tempted you to purchase them in the first place. You've hung onto them only because you hate to give up the extremely valuable storage space that they provide. They refuse to wear out because the construction details are sound, but the style and design leave a lot to be desired. These "monstrosities" are ideal candidates for

If you make an exhaustive search at house sales, country auctions, and thrift shops, you may be able to rescue an old icebox like the one below. Paint it a bright color and set it on the patio. The ice chest is ideal for holding charcoal, and the food compartment can hide the barbecue grill. As an extra safety precaution, drill air holes in the back. The cost will depend on your bargaining skill.

restyling and, given the proper treatment, they can be moved up from an inconspicuous spot in the background to a position of prominence.

For example, if you have a china cabinet that's old (but not antique) and lacks character, why not give it a "face-lifting" treatment? First, examine it for soundness. If there are wobbly joints, repair them before you start to give the cabinet its new personality. If it is constructed of fine furniture wood, you will probably want to restore the grain and color it once had. Use liquid sander and steel wool to remove the old finish, and give it a natural wood finish. If the wood has no natural beauty, you can finish it with semigloss enamel or an antique finish in a color that complements the furnishings of the room in which the cabinet will be used. Cover the back of the cabinet with fabric that matches the draperies and replace the wood shelves with ones of glass.

For a built-in look, fit an old desk into an alcove or corner such as under the stairs. If the door panel is damaged, replace it with an aluminum grille. Cleat one or more two-inch thick shelves to the wall above. Cover the tops of desk and shelves with adhesive-backed paper or vinyl. Apply several coats of antique glaze in a favorite color to all desk surfaces. Materials will cost only about $12.

To add a truly distinctive touch to plain wood cupboards, try a treatment similar to the one that is pictured above. Select adhesive-backed paper or vinyl for decorative panels that contrast with the wood in the cupboards. Mark the location for the panel on each door with a template cut to match the lower corners of the doors. Cut the panels to size. Then, separate each panel from the paper backing as you are ready to apply them, and place the lower edge of the panels to fit the template. Work from the center of the panel to the outer edges, gradually smoothing out any air bubbles. The cost for the adhesive-backed material will be about $12.

It's a pleasure to open cupboard doors when the interior is as colorful as the one above. This tissue collage is durable, and costs less than $5 for materials. Stack six or eight sheets of tissue paper, and cut the designs through all the layers at one time. Paint a small area with liquid plastic or clear varnish. Lay the tissue design on top; it will absorb the adhering liquid and become crystal clear.

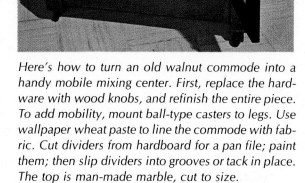

Here's how to turn an old walnut commode into a handy mobile mixing center. First, replace the hardware with wood knobs, and refinish the entire piece. To add mobility, mount ball-type casters to legs. Use wallpaper wheat paste to line the commode with fabric. Cut dividers from hardboard for a pan file; paint them; then slip dividers into grooves or tack in place. The top is man-made marble, cut to size.

Also replace the old hinges and door pulls with hardware that is compatible with the new theme. Your china and crystal will take on new sparkle.

Or you may want to store items that are not really worthy of display in a cabinet that has glass doors. If so, there are many ways to add decorative interest and, at the same time, conceal the contents. You can remove the glass panels and replace them with plastic panels that are semitranslucent, and have the rich appearance of stained glass. You can also use metal mesh, fabric or cane inserts, or louvered shutter panels to replace the panes of glass.

For those of you who have outdated kitchen cupboards, don't be discouraged. You can bring them up-to-date without any great expense. Mount a precast, fiber glass sculptured medallion in the center of each upper door and a narrow sculptured molding around the edge of each door and drawer. (Your paint and lumber supply dealer stocks these in many sizes and designs.) Use paneling adhesive and small nails to attach the medallions and moldings. Paint or antique the cupboards in the color of your choice, then paint the shelves in a contrasting color. Line the backs of the cupboards with vinyl wall covering.

Even the most disreputable old trunks respond like magic to a paint-and-antiquing treatment, and provide you with updated storage space. If you have a trunk tucked away in the basement or attic, get it out and refinish it. Start on yours by giving it a good cleaning and a light sanding. Coat the metal fittings as well as the wood strips and other details with rust-inhibiting paint. Paint the trunk panels with enamel and apply an antique glaze. For a finished look, line the interior with colorful wallpaper that repeats the outside brightness. The trunk not only adds valuable storage space, but it can also serve as an end table or a coffee table. You can even use it to hold components for a home music center— record changer, FM tuner, amplifier, and a clock radio. Use a wire to connect the music center to the speakers located in other parts of the room.

If you have an old wicker trunk or hamper, spray-paint it in a bright color, and you will have a decorative and functional storage space. If the hamper is the tall design, about 12 inches in diameter, you can use it without the lid in the entrance hall for an umbrella stand.

Almost every family has at least one three-drawer chest of undetermined vintage that is scratched and marred from years of service. You can easily remodel this type of chest and give it a completely new look. Cover the top with an 80-inch long piece of ¾-inch plywood. Position one end of the plywood over the chest, and screw it to the chest. Support the far end of the top with a metal bracket fastened to the wall. Give the entire unit an enamel finish, with each of the three drawer fronts a different color. Finish the

task by adding a coat of clear lacquer to add durability, and new brass drawer pulls. You will have a chest-desk unit that will be a welcome addition to any youngster's room.

You can even give a distinctive look to an old mass-produced dresser. If the mirror is attached to the dresser, remove the mounting so that you can hang the mirror on the wall above the dresser when the refinishing is completed. Remove all the hardware before you start. First, sand the existing finish and cut it with benzine. You can achieve an interesting tortoiseshell effect by applying several shades (a different shade for each coat) of a brilliant color that have been diluted with benzine to a watery consistency. It may be necessary to apply four coats to get the desired effect. Let each coat dry before applying the next one. For a subtle gloss, add a coat of clear lacquer. Treat the mirror frame exactly the same way. Spray the hardware with enamel or metallic paint and remount it.

The exterior of the old pine armoire in the living room below was resurfaced with wallpaper. The glass from the doors was removed so that the armoire could be used as a showcase for plants and accessories. The door frame, molding around the top, shelves, and interior were painted the same color as the background in the wallpaper. The wallpaper was sprayed with a coat of clear acrylic in order to make it soil-resistant.

You can create some unexpected storage space by building a bookcase into an ordinary flush door that opens into a closet. This type of built-in requires no valuable space in the living room, yet it is both decorative and functional. Use ¾-inch plywood for the back and sides, and one-inch thick lumber for the shelves. Finish both the interior and the shelves the same as the door itself.

Boots, books, and bags stay put in this inside-the-door storage area. Assign a shelf for each person's gear and plan what goes where in the compartments and drawers. To duplicate this arrangement, order six rectangles (choose two with dividers, and one with drawers) and two squares. Then paint, and stack up. The wall-hung rectangles rest on a 1 x 6 cleat.

BUYING SHELVES AND STORAGE

Not everyone has a supply of items to update. If this is your case, you are probably more interested in shelving units and storage pieces that you can buy for less than $100—and the space organizers that cost only a few dollars. When economy is a factor, the selection of these items in the fine furniture category is limited, but the variety of unfinished, wicker, metal, and thrift shop or auction storage pieces is unlimited.

Shelves and shelving units can be freestanding or wall-hung. They may consist of shelves alone, or a combination of shelves with drawers, cupboards, and/or desk units. Any of the freestanding units can be arranged against a wall or be placed to serve as room dividers.

(1) Freestanding shelf units, since they are made from three basic components—shelves, spindles, and dowel connectors—can be assembled easily without any tools. The shelves come with a hole in each corner to accommodate the threaded dowels that connect the spindles. The spindles are hardwood turnings that come in 22-, 16-, 10-, and 4-inch lengths in designs that harmonize with any style of furnishings. They are unfinished and can be painted, stained, or antiqued. You can assemble these spindles to fit any wall space, use as many shelves as you need, and space the shelves to accommodate the objects you will place on them. The shelves cost about $5 each, and spindles range from about 69¢ to $3 each.

Beautiful, tall, freestanding bookcases in warm-hued finishes that sell for less than $100 each are also available. Measuring 24½ x 11 x 76 inches, they can be used singly or in pairs.

Strong steel shelving units with the shelves finished to simulate the look of fine furniture walnut grain are priced under $20 and come in several sizes. The shelves are adjustable to hold TVs, stereos, books, and other accessories.

If you want, you can combine two or three different sized units to fill an entire wall. The steel uprights have sleek contemporary styling. Free-standing wood shelving is more expensive than is the metal version, but it is still in the economy price range. It makes a handsome addition to traditional or country-style furnishings.

Versatile, heavy-duty steel shelving is very inexpensive and extremely useful for utility purposes. Use this type of shelving in the garage, in the workshop, or in the laundry room. It costs from $5 to $7 for a four-shelf unit. You can add glamour to these units if you cover the shelves with fabric or a wall covering. Do this before assembling, then touch up the screws with paint that matches the color of the covering.

There are also steel shelving units that have black wrought iron, scrollwork uprights in Mediterranean styling. No tools or hardware are needed to assemble them; just snap the units together. Cost is $15 to $25, depending on size.

Unfinished bookcases and shelving units are available in many sizes at budget prices. You can paint or antique them, or give them a natural wood finish. Built of clear pine, they are sanded and all ready to finish as you choose. Bookcases with three shelves are priced from $15 to $20, according to the width of the bookcase.

Shelves and shelving units that are supported by spring-action plungers on the poles can be used against a wall, or as a room divider. The poles extend from 7-foot 6-inches to 8-foot 3-inches in height; extensions are available for higher ceilings. These units come in metal or wood, and in designs that are compatible with any style of furnishings. The shelves are adjustable to fit your individual needs. The entire unit can be moved, removed, or rearranged easily. The least expensive units are made of metal — a four-shelf unit costs less than $15. A single suspension-type pole with three wire racks attached to hold record albums costs only about

The wood shelves that rest on the cabinet base in the photo below are castoff wine racks that were salvaged from a liquor store that was being torn down. Both the cabinet base and the racks were refinished with an antiquing kit. New decorative brass door pulls replaced the old hardware. This bookcase-storage cabinet is as practical as it is unique. Be on the lookout for wine racks such as these when you visit resale shops, and when you attend auctions.

The wall arrangement below consists of three ready-built, unfinished hanging cabinets grouped together. First, the backs of the cabinets were removed and covered with fabric. Then, the cabinets were painted with two coats of enamel. After the paint was dry, the backs (with lining showing) were nailed back on. The cabinets were attached to the walls with screws through the backs into the wall studs. This wall grouping cost approximately $70.

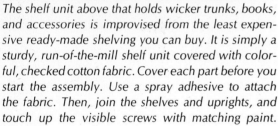

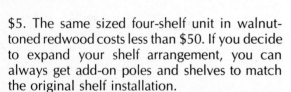

The shelf unit above that holds wicker trunks, books, and accessories is improvised from the least expensive ready-made shelving you can buy. It is simply a sturdy, run-of-the-mill shelf unit covered with colorful, checked cotton fabric. Cover each part before you start the assembly. Use a spray adhesive to attach the fabric. Then, join the shelves and uprights, and touch up the visible screws with matching paint.

You can stretch storage to the ceiling with the desk unit above. Start with a ready-made, unfinished desk unit. Add a back panel of plywood and cover it with cork. Build a simple boxlike light shield to house a long fluorescent bulb. Add three metal shelf standards to reach to the ceiling. Clip in shelf brackets, and cut lengths of 1 x 8s for shelves. Paint the whole unit with two coats of enamel. Cost: about $76.

$5. The same sized four-shelf unit in walnut-toned redwood costs less than $50. If you decide to expand your shelf arrangement, you can always get add-on poles and shelves to match the original shelf installation.

(2) Wall-hung shelving is available to suit every pocketbook, every room, and every style of furnishings. It ranges from the least expensive laminated surface hardboard and metal shelves supported by aluminum or wrought iron brackets and standards to dramatically sculptured wood shelves mounted on pilasters or brackets of classic design. There are even small corner shelves that can hold a single, important decorative item. Wall-hung units may be the perfect solution for you; but remember that dismantling and rehanging them involves a lot of work.

Hand-woven, imported wicker shelves in natural or painted finishes are at home in any style of furnishings. Wrought iron shelves that feature swirling scrolls and a rich black finish are especially appropriate for displaying accessories with a Mediterranean flair. Glass shelves that rest on slim, shiny metal legs add a modern touch with their see-through look.

A console table, actually nothing more than a small shelf mounted to a wall, is a practical and decorative asset in an entrance hall. Hang a mirror above it, and arrange one or two accessories on it. Many of these small, decorative shelves are replicas of hand-carved originals. You can find them in wood tones or metallic finishes. Some have marble tops; others, man-made marble tops. Prices vary according to design.

If you're short on storage space for dishes and glassware that you use frequently, you can install a notched board to hold stemware. Simply insert each piece of stemware upside down in a notch so that it is supported by the base. This idea was borrowed from a restaurant, where it is important to reach pieces quickly. The shelf below holds dishes. Both shelves are stained in a wood tone, and positioned for convenience.

You can purchase a wrought iron rack like the one above for less than $5. This type is ordinarily used in kitchens to hold utensils, but here it is used in a man's dressing area to hold ties. The rugged metal frame adapts well to a masculine theme, and its many hooks make it possible to see at a glance the selection of neckwear available. The metal frame can be spray-painted whenever you decide to change the color scheme.

Avoid kitchen clutter by buying inexpensive ready-made shelves and brackets and installing above the kitchen counter. Get six-inch wide shelves so they won't extend too far over the work surface. Paint them to match the wall color. Arrange most-used items so they are readily accessible, and intersperse them with a few decorative items. Add hooks beneath the shelves for hanging gadgets where they can be reached.

The tall rattan bookcases below are so versatile that they can be used in any room in the home. They are hand-woven and imported. Here, they are shown in the natural finish, but they can be spray-painted in any color that harmonizes with surrounding furnishings. They are a pleasing complement to furnishings of other materials — wood, metal, or glass. Wicker and rattan furniture is available in a wide selection of storage pieces — free-standing and wall-hung shelves and bookcases, chests, hampers, and trunks. Prices vary according to size and quality; the ones below cost well under $100 each.

Here's a shelving and storage unit that will serve as a hobby center for your entire family. There's ample room for collections, accessories, greenery, stereo components, TV, and lots of books. The entire unfinished unit, including the hardwood turnings, shelves, and wood connectors, costs about $70. No tools are necessary to join them together. The spindles, available in the classic, traditional, or Americana styles, come in 22-, 16-, 10-, and 4-inch lengths, and can be combined in an arrangement that fits your needs. The unit can be either painted or stained to suit your decorating theme.

The shelf and storage unit above is a simple arrangement. Start with an unfinished three-drawer chest and a slab door for the desk. Use 2 x 4s for the framework, with boards laid across wherever you want shelf space. This is an ideal unit for a boy's bedroom. It is sturdy, has lots of shelf and storage space, and provides a study area. Paint it in bright colors to accent the room's furnishings, and mount a lamp above the desk.

Storage pieces include a large number of items such as cabinets or cupboards, chests, or any one of a myriad of space-extended racks, rods, poles, and containers. Also included are outdoor storage units—a small shed to house the trash can, gardening supplies, or barbecue equipment; or even a bicycle rack. Their primary function is to help the homemaker solve storage problems, but, at the same time, they can also fill a niche in the total decorating plan.

Even though your budget may not permit you to splurge on a storage piece of fine cabinet wood, you can still purchase an item that will fill that important storage space need. You can always add a stamp of individuality to an inexpensive ready-to-finish cabinet or chest by painting or antiquing it yourself. And since wicker furniture is no longer confined to porches, patios, and sunrooms, it has taken on new significance

in the decorating world. You can buy wicker chests, cabinets, hampers, trunks, and baskets for storage. They make handsome additions in their natural finish, or they can be spray-painted.

Basically, a cabinet or cupboard is any large off-the-floor box that has doors and shelves, and is supported by legs or mounted on the wall. Within this broad classification there are china cabinets, armoires, kitchen cabinets, file cabinets, and cabinets that house sewing equipment, liquor, guns, records and tapes, and medicine.

A chest is simply a large box with legs that raise it off the floor. When there are a number of small boxes encased within the big box, they become drawers—thus, the name chest of drawers. Regardless of size, design, and type of material used in construction, their purpose remains the same as it was thousands of years ago when ancient coffers were used to store precious

belongings. Chests of drawers, cedar chests, toy chests, silverware chests that are compartmented and lined with tarnishproof material, jewelry chests lined with silk or velvet, and tool chests are all included in this category.

Other storage pieces that are useful in any home are wastebaskets, magazine racks, luggage racks, desks, and serving carts. If you have a fireplace in your home, you will want a basket to hold the logs and a rack for fireplace tools.

In addition to the unfinished storage pieces in country-style or modern design that have been on the market for some time, you can now get ready-to-finish chests, trunks, and desks in the popular campaign style. Even though they are inspired by the collapsible furniture that military officers carried with them from one battlefield to another, modern adaptations are geared to fill the needs of space-conscious homemakers. They can be mixed or stacked in a variety of space-

If you're a knitting enthusiast and need a convenient place to store your yarn, use a plastic shoe bag. You can hang it on the back of a closet door, or on the closet pole. The contents are clearly visible through the see-through plastic, and are kept dust-free. These handy storage bags cost less than $3, and can also be used to store many other items in an orderly fashion.

You can create an eye-stopping storage unit in an entryway by stacking together four columns of cubes. The cubes measure 16-inches square, and come unfinished. Concealed wood strips tie the cubes together. You don't need to fasten them to the floor or wall. Paint them whatever color you wish, and arrange books, magazines, and accessories on the shelves.

You can create an all-family work center by assembling stack units of un-finished chests and shelves. Use a wide slab door for the work table. Support it with 2 x 2 legs at one end; cleat the other end to the wall. Organize the units into the best arrangement, and top with a single piece of ¾-inch plywood. The hanging gun rack is another inexpensive, ready-to-finish storage piece, painted to match the color of the work center.

saving arrangements. These items come fully assembled except for the brass-toned metal hardware which is easier to attach after the finishing treatment. Campaign furniture lends itself well to a wood-tone finish or a high-gloss enamel finish.

(1) Multipurpose furniture with storage compartments is a wise choice for any room in your home. Manufacturers recognize the need for furniture that fills more than one requirement and, as a result, offer a constantly expanding line in all furniture styles and in a wide price range.

This category, too, includes a variety of items. There are occasional, coffee, and end tables with shelves and/or drawers below; some have racks below to hold record albums or magazines. Bedside chests can double as night stands, and a headboard with open shelves or sliding door panels can hold books, a clock, and a radio. There are chests with open shelves above, and there are desk-chest units. Some chests are compartmented to hold records and tapes, and

stereo components; others open to reveal a refreshment center with a working area top protected by a plastic laminate surface.

Cubes with hinged tops can take the place of small tables or add extra seating and, at the same time, provide storage space within. A serving cart with drop leaves, and shelves or drawers below, can hold items for entertaining. Benches with storage compartments are ideal for hiding extra bedding. A bedroom chair that doubles as a valet rack and has a lift-up seat for storing accessories is greatly appreciated by the man of the house. Even bookshelves and cabinets can fill two important needs if used as room dividers as well as storage units.

(2) Kitchen storage is one of the simplest problems with which to cope, and one of the least expensive, if you have even a modest amount of built-in cupboard space to start with. Efficient organization and planning are much more important than the amount of money you spend.

Not everything you use can be kept right at your fingertips, but those items you use daily should be most conveniently placed. Those used less frequently can be stored in the less accessible areas. The size of a family and its pattern of living will determine which items deserve prime position in the kitchen cupboards.

If your countertop work area space is limited, try to keep it free of small appliances and other necessary equipment. You can save valuable space if your hand mixer and can opener are wall-mounted. You can hang small shelves above the counter to hold the toaster, canister set, salt and pepper shakers, and spices.

If you can part with a few inches of space between the countertop and the cupboards above, you can mount tilt-out drawers to the bottoms of the cupboards. Use one drawer for kitchen gadgets and cutlery, one for spices and condiments, and another for rolls of foil and food wrap. There are dinnerware racks that hold a service of eight in a minimum amount of shelf space,

and shelf extenders that literally double cupboard space. Adjustable dividers for drawers can partition the space so that none is wasted.

One of the best places to add storage space is on the backs of doors. You can use the back of a closet door, one that goes to the basement, or one that opens into the utility room. Even your cupboard doors may be large enough to have a rack mounted on the back. If it's a tall door, you can mount three racks, one above another. Use a file-type rack at the top to hold grocery or storage bags; a wrap-bag organizer in the middle to hold foil, food wrap, and baggies; and at the bottom a caddy with a towel bar to hold cleaning supplies. Steel shelf units that adjust from 14 to 24 inches wide and have 6 shelves with guards to help protect stored items are also available. These can be mounted on the back of a door, or wall-hung to hold canned goods.

Once you've decided just what type of storage will be the most valuable to you, shop in housewares departments for space-saving aids.

The desk below can grow with a child, year after year. It is made simply by assembling ready-to-finish stack units, and a two-foot wide slab door for the desk top. Here, the desk top is 30 inches high. For a small child, the door can be placed between the stacked base units at a 15-inch height. Paint the desk-storage combination a bright color, and mount a square piece of cork covered with felt above the desk for use as a bulletin board.

BUILDING SHELVES AND STORAGE

Once you've mentally resolved your storage problems—where you need additional storage units, and what type will be the most helpful—it's up to you to decide just how much time, energy, and money you want to invest in the project. If you own your own home, you may want to invest in permanent built-in units; if you are a renter, freestanding units may be the answer; and if you're part of the mobile society that relocates frequently, you may want units that can be easily assembled and reassembled.

There are many types of storage units that feature simple construction details and inexpensive materials; what's more, they are not too complicated for the home handyman to tackle. There are times when ordinary wooden shelves will ease the storage pressures, and these are not difficult for the novice to attempt. Even those people who claim to have no carpentry skills can learn to mount panels of perforated hardboard where items can hang from hooks.

You may have a workshop stocked with tools, but if you haven't, don't think you have to go out and buy expensive power tools before you start a simple project. All you need are a hammer, saw, screw driver, and pliers. You can rent a power saw or drill for a day, or for a weekend. However, if you find out later that you're going to be using tools of this type frequently, that is the time to invest in power tools.

Shelves are often as easy to build as storage units. These mounted units are a welcome addition to any room in the home, as well as in the garage, basement, or even the patio. The boards

A handsome shelf like the one below can be tailored to fit the space requirements in any home, using inch-and-a-half-thick lumber. Cut the edge design with a shaper or router, have the brackets made at an ornamental ironwork shop. Screw the brackets to the studs. Paint the shelves, and use the same color in accessories, and fabric for cushions on the stools. Finish the shelf with a coat of clear lacquer. The materials for this attractive shelf cost about $28.50.

The storage cabinet below is 18 inches deep, 48 inches wide, and ceiling height. Install a 30-watt fluorescent fixture to light the interior. To hold the removable acrylic panels to inside of doors, tack ⅛-inch rabbeted molding around the sides and bottom. Paint the cabinet and shelves the same as the background color of the wall covering. Top the adjacent breakfast bar with plastic laminate covering. The cost of all the materials is a little less than $100.

This unit will ease the storage problem and, at the same time, make the man of the house happy. Build the base cabinet first, and fit it with slide-out trays for folded clothes. Plan the width for available space; make it 36 inches high, and from 20 to 24 inches deep. Build the upper unit to the ceiling and about 12 inches deep. Add plywood shelves, and a tie rack; use louvered shutter doors for the upper unit. Paint the entire unit. Materials will cost around $50.

If you have a seldom-used closet that is adjacent to the family room, you can convert it into a compact music center, complete with built-in shelves and cabinets. Here, colorful flocked wallpaper covers the ceiling as well as the walls, with matching paint used on all wood surfaces. A folding panel door conceals the music center when it's not in use. A wall light brightens the area for record selection and changer operation. This built-in costs about $70.

Towel bars like those that are pictured below can be planned to fit any amount of wall space in your bathroom. Make the wood supports from walnut. First, cut them to size, then sand the wood supports and drill for bars and bolts. Attach the supports to the wall with toggle bolts or lag screws. The square rods are made of metal, and are available separately at most stores. These towel bars are functional and decorative, and cost only about $30.

What, at first, appears to be a cube table, has a roomy drawer for storing a whole record collection. It is easy to build from fir plywood, and you can cover it with plastic laminate in a bright color. Add the bronze hardware to accent its decorative value. Let it rest on a base slightly smaller than the cube. The materials will cost approximately $18. If you can find a discarded one-drawer file cabinet, you can decorate it in a similar manner.

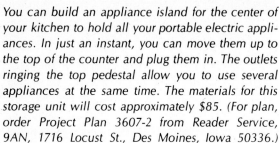

You can build an appliance island for the center of your kitchen to hold all your portable electric appliances. In just an instant, you can move them up to the top of the counter and plug them in. The outlets ringing the top pedestal allow you to use several appliances at the same time. The materials for this storage unit will cost approximately $85. (For plan, order Project Plan 3607-2 from Reader Service, 9AN, 1716 Locust St., Des Moines, Iowa 50336.)

This pull-out pan storage unit resolves any problems that you may have about storing cooking utensils right where they are readily accessible. And, it takes up very little room from your existing cupboard space. Frame ¼-inch perforated hardboard with 1 x 2s, and mount it vertically with drawer glides at the top and bottom. The paneling used on the door matches that of the cupboards. You can build this handy storage unit for your kitchen for about $12.

can be cut to length at the lumberyard to simplify the job. Then, all you have to do is mount the shelves on wall brackets or upright supports.

If you wish, you can even frame a window with bookshelves. Use four ceiling-to-floor length 1 x 12s; mount one on each side of window, the other pair 12 inches from each side of window. Divide the space horizontally as you wish, and mount shelves. Paint the unit in a shiny enamel. The cost for this arrangement: $45.

You can build a spacious serving shelf for about $10. Make a plywood box, 7 feet long, 14 inches wide, and 3½ inches deep, and support it by two steel brackets—one under each end.

To build a simple, but elegant buffet wall, start with a long serving shelf. Use ¾-inch plywood, or a 1 x 12 for the shelf and cover it with

plastic laminate; add shallow drawers for storing table linens and silver. Build smaller shelves 10 inches wide, and mount them above the buffet on shelf standards. The materials needed to build this unit will cost you about $56.

For a child's room, build cupboards with open shelves above to display toys, and sliding doors below to conceal not-so-attractive items. Build the frames from 1 x 8-inch pine boards. Set the frames on bases of 1 x 2s. Cover ⅛-inch hardboard with burlap and nail on over the backs of the frames. Install metal sliding door track and perforated hardboard doors. The material for each large cupboard will cost about $35.

To conceal open shelves, install a window shade or bamboo blind above the shelves that can be raised or lowered easily.

A server that can take its place in either a dining room, or a kitchen is made simply by assembling components. The open shelves at either end started out as unpainted end tables, and the top is a 60 x 30-inch flush door. The top is covered with white leatherlike plastic material, and the tables are painted a psychedelic green. A wicker wine rack, painted the same green, rests on top of the server, and a wall hanging balances the tall wine rack.

You can fill an entire wall with shuttered base cabinets for needed storage, and open shelves above to display an interesting assortment of collector pieces. These storage pieces and stack units are available ready to finish at most building supply dealers. You will gain quite a lot of decorating impact by painting the cabinets in colors that appear in the patterned wall covering. It will cost you slightly less than $100 to build the entire unit.

It doesn't take a lot of power tools, and a lot of time to build this simple bookcase and desk unit. You can build the bookcase out of 1 x 10 lumber (have the boards cut to length at the building supply dealer), and space the dividers close enough together to provide the necessary support. Nail in a slanted shelf to hold magazines. Build the desk so that one end rests on the bookcase. The materials for this bookcase unit can be purchased for about $50.

Here's a way to break up a large expanse of wall and gain valuable storage space at the same time. This 16-inch deep unit is five feet wide, and extends from floor to ceiling. The boxed end panels are made of ¼-inch plywood over 2 x 4 frames. The open shelves above provide display area for books and colorful accessories, while the doors below offer storage space for records, games, and items you want to conceal. Materials for this unit will cost about $37.

ORGANIZING STORAGE SPACE

Most homemakers agree that there is never enough storage space in the home, regardless of its size. More often than not, the problem is not so much a lack of storage facilities as it is one of inefficient use of existing storage space. You can overcome this by using space organizers.

These handy items can be found in houseware and closet accessory departments. For a kitchen, there are dish racks that hold a service for eight in a very small space, and adjustable shelf ex-

tenders that fit any cupboard. Use a lazy susan in that hard-to-reach corner cupboard, and dividers in the drawers. To increase closet storage space, there are complete closet organizers that you can install quickly and easily. These have adjustable rods, shelves, and hooks, and can be assembled to fit individual needs and preferences.

Whether you solve your storage problems by updating some of the furniture pieces you already have, or by purchasing or building shelves and storage units, additional storage space can be yours—inexpensively and easily.

Midway shelves actually double cupboard storage space. You can move shelves up or down, or remove them, whenever your space requirements change.

Store your paper products in one or two of these little units you can build to fit neatly in your existing cabinets. Made from scrap plywood, it costs only $8.

You can build this closet door valet for $8. Buy a medicine chest, aluminum tubing, four right angle fittings, and four flange fittings. Make tubing into two brackets; screw to door. Bolt cabinet on brackets.

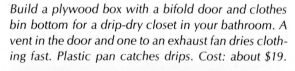

Build a plywood box with a bifold door and clothes bin bottom for a drip-dry closet in your bathroom. A vent in the door and one to an exhaust fan dries clothing fast. Plastic pan catches drips. Cost: about $19.

Shallow slide-out trays provide maximum storage space for canned goods. You can see at a glance the exact contents of each shelf. Allow more space between the trays at the bottom for larger sizes of goods.

Mount a sturdy wire utility basket on the back of the cupboard door below the sink in your kitchen. This provides easy access to the most-used cleaning materials, and keeps them neatly arranged.

Vegetable bins, that are simply large wire baskets, slide in and out on drawer glides. Contents are clearly visible. This is a good example of making the best possible use of the storage space you have.

Swing-out spice shelves like those below make it possible to tell at a glance what is in each container, and to keep spice jars neatly arranged. This provides four tiers of shelves in the same amount of space that ordinarily contains two shelves. Narrow wood strips prevent jars from being dislodged.

Here, a white traditional bathroom vanity trimmed in gold has unexpected storage facilities behind the doors below. Tote trays, for each member of the family, glide in and out easily and hold personal grooming necessities. The shelf trays in the center hold a large supply of bathroom linens.

You can dress up a simple box spring
and mattress combination with an
inexpensive, decorative headboard.
It can be as simple as a sheet of
prefinished wood paneling or a panel
of fabric attached to the wall, or as
elegant as a custom-built version
with shelves and storage units built in.

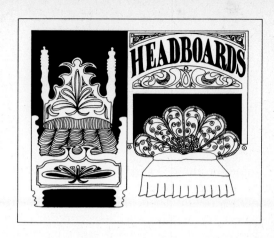

HEADBOARDS

Is it possible to furnish or refurnish your bedroom and still balance that ever-present, better-not-stretch-me budget? The answer is "yes." And if you are resourceful, you can incorporate both beauty and comfort into your decor.

The bed, of course, is the single, most important item in any bedroom. So it makes sense that the biggest portion of the decorating budget be allotted to the purchase of a spring and mattress.

But a new bed alone, no matter how expensive, won't give you that "new room" look you are striving for. So, why not buy or make a headboard that harmonizes with the mood of the room, and the furnishings that surround it?

Deciding what kind of headboard you want to purchase and just how much you want to spend for it are up to you and your budget. If you have visions of an elegant, delicately carved headboard, but simply can't afford it now, don't dismiss the idea completely. Instead, simply attach a panel of inexpensive fabric to the wall behind the bed. Let the panel serve as a headboard until the time comes that you can replace it with the headboard of your choice.

If you decide to buy a headboard, look at all the styles and materials available before making your choice. Remember that although the headboard doesn't have to match the other furnishings, it should be scaled to the size of the room, and its color should blend with accessories in the room.

There are Victorian design wicker headboards that are at home with any style of furnishings; wood headboards with panel inserts of cane or metal mesh, brass headboards, and many others.

If you really want to save some money, you can make your own headboard. This is an easy project for the home handyman, and the variety of designs is enormous. For example, in a boy's room, a headboard covered with leatherlike fabric that can withstand hard wear may be what you need.

HEADBOARDS YOU CAN MAKE

When making your own headboard, creative talent and inventiveness are much more important than is the amount of money you spend. First, decide whether you want a formal or informal mood; and whether you want the headboard to have a modern look, or one of earlier origin. Then, decide which material— wood, metal, fabric, leather, cork, or carpet— you want to use. Even a grouping of framed prints can give a headboard effect.

If you want to inject a note of nostalgia, look around for old items that you can convert into headboards. An old brass bedstead, for example, can be cleaned, polished, and given a coat of clear lacquer. Or an iron bedstead that has been discarded can be sanded, and enameled in the color of your choice. Even a wrought iron gate or section of fence, rescued from a brownstone that is being demolished, can be painted and used as a headboard. For a really unique headboard, find some weathered barn siding boards and join them together with black iron strap hinges, or leather harness straps. A headboard of this type is sure to capture the spotlight in a bedroom with country-style furnishings.

Did you know that your monstrous, old oak headboard, that at first glance seems so grotesque, can be cut down to a size that doesn't dwarf the other furnishings in the room? You can refinish, enamel, or antique it. For a luxurious look, you can even tuft it. First, cut half-inch thick upholstery foam to fit the size and shape of

You can create a wall-wide headboard by covering the wall sections with black felt, and repeating it in the scalloped-edge cornice ornamented with black and white braid and yarn tassels. For bold contrast, backdrop the bed with white floor-length curtains. This treatment costs about $55.

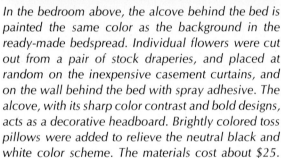

In the bedroom above, the alcove behind the bed is painted the same color as the background in the ready-made bedspread. Individual flowers were cut out from a pair of stock draperies, and placed at random on the inexpensive casement curtains, and on the wall behind the bed with spray adhesive. The alcove, with its sharp color contrast and bold designs, acts as a decorative headboard. Brightly colored toss pillows were added to relieve the neutral black and white color scheme. The materials cost about $25.

The graceful wicker headboard and pair of bedside tables, spray-painted white, add a cheerful note in the little girl's bedroom above. The canopy above is just as easy to make as curtains or draperies. Tack a 1 x 2 wood strip to the ceiling and attach the canopy fabric with tiny staples. Pleat the fabric at the top with the same button treatment used in the draperies that are barely visible at the left. Wicker headboards cost about $25, and you can build the canopy with about $10 worth of materials.

the headboard. Leave about two inches of wood showing around the edge for a border, glue the foam in place. Cover the foam with fabric, and tuft it. Tack the fabric in place with small nails, and edge with a braid in a matching color.

If you have a portable headboard in mind, use a three- or four-panel, ready-made folding screen with fiberboard panels. First, paint or finish the frames; then, cover the panels with patterned fabric, wallpaper, wet-look or wood-grain vinyl wall covering, felt, or burlap. In a girl's bedroom, you might want to cover the panels with felt in a vivid color and attach Valentines or prom programs to alternate panels. In a boy's room, try covering the panels with burlap, and glue on photos of sports events.

In a bedroom with a contemporary theme, you can make a headboard from a sheet of pre-

finished oak paneling. Fasten the paneling to the wall and add lengths of pine molding (sanded and painted) at either side. Buy a pair of small, unfinished cabinets and hang them on the wall at either side of the bed instead of using night stands. Paint the cabinets the same color as the pine molding strips and use the leftover pieces of the oak paneling to make sliding doors for the cabinets. For good reading light, hang ceiling fixtures at a height that gives adequate light.

For an inexpensive canopy effect, apply vinyl wall covering the same width as the bed all the way up the wall and extend it for several feet onto the ceiling. Outline the headboard-canopy with a border of two-inch wide vinyl tape in a contrasting color. This is an ideal treatment for a small bedroom, as it creates a dramatic effect without taking up valuable floor space.

Crisp blue and white checked gingham in a mini-scale check forms the canopy, side curtains, and cafe curtains in the teen-ager's combination bed-sitting room above. The bright wallpaper print is used on the ceiling, as a wider border, and as a backdrop for the bed. The canopy and side curtains, louvered shutters painted white, patterned wall, and bright red bolsters that match the coverlet combine to give the effect of a massive headboard. White wall fixtures are conveniently mounted at each side of the studio bed. The same checked gingham is used for a dust ruffle, and to cover several toss pillows.

You can design a headboard and can have it made to your exact specifications at a millwork shop. The finished headboard should extend slightly beyond the bed frame on either side. Assemble the pieces against the wall, and carefully mark the position of each piece. Nail each firmly to the wall studs with large finish nails. Fill all the nail holes, and stain the completed headboard unit. The one above cost approximately $75. If you prefer, the headboard could be painted, or antiqued in whatever color complements the furnishings in your bedroom. The design can be as simple, or as elegant as you wish it to be.

The fabric on the headboard below is simply a large, soft-touch towel. Make a frame with width of a twin bed, using 1⅜-inch wide corner bead. Cut ⅜-inch plywood to fit inside the frame and serve as a backing. Baste towel to padding cut to size to fit the backing. Cover buttons, and sew to the towel through padding. Staple towel to plywood and fasten in frame. Paint corner bead to match towel colors. Materials cost about $20.

The headboard in the bedroom above is nothing more than a swath of heavy cotton fabric that extends across the entire wall above the bed and bedside tables. The length of fabric, with its bold designs and vivid colors, is tacked to a frame made of 2 x 2s. The whole headboard is light enough to hang just as you would a picture.

You can create a headboard to display your favorite photos. Make a frame slightly wider than the width of the bed and 18 inches high. Cover the backboard with some of the bedspread fabric. You can duplicate this type of headboard treatment for about $25. Whenever you want a change, rearrange the pictures or add new ones.

The headboard above is blue felt applied to the wall from floor to ceiling. Use white glue, thinned slightly with water. Spread solution on wall with a brush and let it dry until it is tacky. Press felt in place, trim excess. Cost: about $33. A wall hanging, mounted horizontally, emphasizes the headboard effect and adds contrast.

This type of headboard works especially well in a low-ceilinged room such as the one below (this bedroom is in a finished attic with a hipped ceiling). The headboard is made of ordinary foam pillows covered with cotton velveteen; they are suspended from a length of wood closet pole. You can buy the wooden support brackets to hold the pole, and the decorative end finials in any drapery department. For a final touch, add a decorative pillow made of the same velveteen. Install one hook on the wall, and another one on the ceiling to hold the cord and chain for the swag lamp that hangs directly over the night stand.

Here's a headboard-canopy over a sofa bed that will delight any small child. Besides, it's inexpensive, and easy to make. Cut strips of felt four inches wide and eight feet long. Hang the poles (wood closet poles that are painted) with cord that hangs from the ceiling. Drape the felt strips over the poles uniformly. Felt is especially suited to this type of treatment because it is not necessary to finish the edges. Alternate strips of three or four different colors, and repeat the colors in pillows, decorative accessories, and wall hangings. This bed canopy will only cost about $14 for the materials you need.

Plan your lighting to achieve visual comfort, to create
the mood and atmosphere you desire, and to enhance the
colors of your background and furnishings. Combine
background, local, and accent lighting to give balanced
illumination that is restful to the eye and
that is flattering to the furnishings in your home.

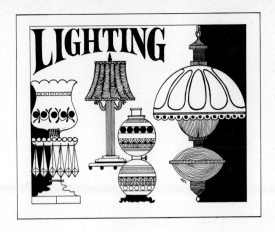

LIGHTING FIXTURES & LAMPS

Well-planned lighting is a valuable asset —one that you can't afford to do without. Good lighting not only highlights the colors of your furnishings, but it also adds convenience to your daily living. At times, good lighting is overlooked when decorating plans are made. If this happens to you, remember that there are many ways to improve lighting.

There are three basic types of lighting: background (or general), local, and accent. Each of these types of lighting is necessary to provide even illumination.

Background lighting (ceiling and wall fixtures) provides soft general illumination. Built-in lighting is one form of background lighting and includes lighted cornices, coves, wall brackets, valances, and lighted soffits.

Local lighting provides light for reading, sewing, writing, and dozens of other specialized interests. This type of lighting is most often supplied by lamps and suspended wall fixtures or ceiling fixtures placed close to the user.

Accent lighting is used to highlight an important wall grouping or painting, or a furniture grouping.

Take a good look at each room in your home to see where lighting should be improved, or added. Remember that lighting requirements vary from room to room. Living rooms need background, local, and accent lighting. Dining rooms need local lighting for serving purposes, and background lighting for atmosphere. Bedrooms need background lighting, plus local lighting for reading. Kitchens and bathrooms both need strong illumination. There should also be a sufficient number of outlets for every room (two for each 12 feet of wall space) and appliance, conveniently spaced all through your home.

Lighting fixtures of all types are available in styles to complement any furnishings. If your budget is limited, put your imagination to work and make your own lighting fixtures and lamps, or adapt those you have to suit your needs.

You can build this hanging light fixture from a wire fish-keeper. First, remove top and bottom circular traps from keeper and reattach one with wire two inches from bottom. Spray-paint mesh black. Make a cylindrical tube of white vinyl-coated lampshade material. Cut material to size, form a tube, and fasten with white glue. Insert tube into keeper. Next, place light socket, with ample white electrical cord, inside of tube and knot cord where it comes out top of tube. At the knot, wire cord in middle of keeper. Cut, sand, and paint an arm of wood, drilling holes at front and back to slip cord through.

FIXTURES AND LAMPS TO MAKE

Your home can reflect a welcoming light if you make your own lighting fixtures and lamps. All the individual pieces—harps for lamps, wire, plugs, and sockets—are available at lamp shops for the home hobbyist who wants to create interesting and unusual lighting fixtures and lamps.

This is true, too, for outdoor fixtures that light up the entryway. You can build one with a cylinder of glass or plastic for about $8. Simply drill a hole in the back for wiring, and fasten to the wall. Glue on colored glass squares, available at hobby shops, and fill in between squares with mastic. Then, add the wiring.

But you must combine the decorative aspect of a lamp with its function. Another unique fixture for an entryway is made of decorative clay flowerpots and saucers. Stack various sized pots and saucers in an arrangement that suits you, and space them apart with wood blocks. Then, run the wiring through holes in the bottoms of the pots. The cost is about $18.

It's just as easy to make indoor lamps. Make an oriental-type hanging light fixture that is appropriate in a room with a contemporary theme for about $22. Use paper lanterns of several sizes—both round and cylindrical shapes—and join them, one above another, in an imaginative design. Glue the edges together, or sew them together with thin wire wrapped around the wooden frames. Use a string of Christmas lights with low wattage, white frosted bulbs inside. Hang the fixture from a ceiling hook and run the wire down a corner to an outlet.

Lamp bases also can be made from many different items, and topped with an inexpensive shade. A tall vase or pitcher, an old, upright telephone, a milk can, a coffee grinder, or an earthenware jug are all objects that lend themselves to lamp conversion, and add a bit of nostalgia to a room with country-style furnishings.

A pop-art wastebasket that costs about $1.50 can also be wired and become a lamp base. These bigger-than-life pop cans, flashlight batteries, beer cans, and popcorn cans add a lively touch to a family room, or to a teen-ager's room. Use a colorful burlap shade from a variety store.

If you have an old table lamp with no particular design features, paint the base, or cover it with raffia, gluing it as you wrap it around. Or glue on mosaic tiles, stones, or shells.

Build this outdoor wooden light for about $15. Saw ½ x 6 cedar paneling into ¼ x ¾-inch strips. Nail 4-inch wide pieces to make 6¼-inch square for bottom sections — allowing overlap of 2 inches at top, 8 inches at bottom. Saw corner strips 40 inches long so they can be buried in ground. Install waterproof light socket in base.

You can make this 12-inch diameter elegant glass tile globe for about $23. Buy a glass (or plastic) globe in an electrical supply store, and apply mosaic glass tiles to the surface, using white glue as the adhesive. Four square feet of tile will cover this size globe. Mosaic tiles are sold at most hobby shops and building supply dealers.

This octagonal-shaped bedroom night stand, 12 inches wide by 23 inches high, requires ¾ foot of filigree hardboard. Bevel slightly on vertical cut edges of each 4½-inch wide panel. Make the base and the top of 1 x 2s or ¾-inch plywood. Conceal the edges of the top and bottom with a ¼ x 1¼-inch rim.

An old ironstone pitcher, a family hand-me-down, was converted into the lamp below. The wiring was done at a lamp shop, where the bronze base was added to give it extra height. The cost for the lamp and white pleated vinyl shade was less than $20.

To light up the patio, convert ordinary kitchen funnels into blooming torches. Insert dowel rods, painted green, into the funnels. Drill holes in the sides of the funnels, paint flower petal designs in bright colors and add multicolored candles.

You can turn a narrow ledge behind the sofa into an exciting display area when light comes from a recessed panel. Make light box at least six inches deep and center a single fluorescent tube toward top. Recess a translucent plastic panel so that it is level with top of enclosure; let it just rest there to facilitate cleaning and tube-changing. You can use the same idea with bookshelves under the cavity.

Soffit lighting solves the doubly complicated problem of how to attractively illuminate a bath and still provide maximum light. Build the soffit as long and wide as the counter and about eight inches deep. Install two rows of tubes if the soffit is standard 18 inches wide; three rows if it's more. Use a lightly etched or figured diffuser if you don't require maximum brightness; a louvered diffuser if you do.

Built-in lighting—cornices, valances, coves, wall brackets, and soffits—is a good source of general lighting that can be built into your home without a great deal of expense. Every room has some area that will benefit from a built-in unit.

(**1**) Cornices direct all their light downward to give dramatic interest to wall coverings.

(**2**) Valances are always used at windows, usually with draperies. They provide up-light, which reflects off the ceiling for general room lighting, and down-light for drapery accent.

(**3**) Coves direct all light to the ceiling, and should be used only with white or near-white ceilings. Use them to supplement other lighting.

(**4**) Brackets. High wall brackets provide both up- and down-light for general room lighting. Low wall brackets are used for special emphasis.

(**5**) Soffits for bathrooms and dressing rooms are designed to light the user's face. They are almost always used with large mirrors.

You can build this double-duty shelf light for about $16. Just build a box from hardwood or pine with the bottom slanted slightly to the back. Use a piece of translucent plastic for a bottom panel and leave a one-inch gap between the front panel and edge of top. Screw 30-watt fluorescent fixture to back. This gives you even, eye-soothing fluorescent light, plus a good looking display area for accessories.

Add custom-made charm to an inexpensive lamp shade with freshly picked, flattened flowers. Lay out fern and small flowers in desired pattern, and place on shade. Mix one part transparent glue with two parts water. Smear liberally on 3 x 5-inch sheets of rice paper. Then, press sheets over floral composition. Blooms will keep their natural color. Cost: under $5.

Trimming lamp shades is one of the simplest and least expensive ways to add decorative interest to a room. Most ready-made shades are plastic or silk; either one will lend itself to decorative trim. You can either update the shades you already have, or buy inexpensive ones and add your own custom touch.

Take a plain, unadorned white plastic shade and cover it with fabric that matches the draperies or bedspread. Simply attach the material with double-faced pressure-sensitive tape, keeping the fabric wrinkle-free. Add a border of narrow braid at both the top and bottom edges for a finished look. You can also trim a plain shade by gluing on large, colorful motifs cut from patterned fabric or wall covering.

Take heed of the suggestions that are presented in this chapter concerning lighting fixtures and lamps, and you, too, can combine balanced illumination and beauty in your home lighting—easily and economically.

The paisley-patterned fabric, scaled to giant proportions, is used to cover the lamp shade and cushions in the room below. Use double-faced pressure-sensitive tape to attach the fabric to the lamp shade. You can build a successful color scheme by taking colors from a pattern created by an expert, such as has been done here. In this room, one of the fabric's subtle background colors, white, was used on the painted walls. The medium shade of green was used for the carpet. Still other shades of green appear in the lamp base, and the pieces of painted wicker furniture. Whatever pattern you choose, select the hues you like best from the design; discard the others.

Even though you enjoy plants just for themselves, you can increase your pleasure when you select and arrange greenery so that it provides a delightful accent to the furnishings in your home. Use both foliage and flowering plants. Mass several small plants in one impressive grouping, or display a single, large plant in a prominent location that makes it the center of interest.

GREENERY

You can make any room in your home come alive with the addition of greenery, for houseplants provide maximum beauty with a minimum of expense, and offer endless decorating possibilities.

Whether you choose foliage or flowering plants, or a combination of the two, greenery is the perfect finishing touch to any room. A single plant can rest on a coffee table or mantel; a hanging basket of ivy adds life to a gleaming bathroom; and a terrarium fits in well with the lively furnishings in a child's room. Groups of plants can be arranged in a bay window, on a wide window ledge or a radiator top, or even on a teacart.

When choosing plants, follow the same decorating principles as you would in the selection of other furnishings—size, form, color, and texture. Also, be sure to consider the style of furnishings you have. Large plants with shiny leaves are ideal for contemporary rooms with slim, sleek furnishings, while other plants with leaves that have a lacelike look are often more at home in traditional or country-style surroundings.

Don't let the size of your rooms curb your enthusiasm for greenery. Even in a small room or entryway, a tall plant takes up very little floor space and contributes a great deal of interest. A large expanse of wall needs a plant or group of plants of the same proportions. To show off your plants most effectively, they should not be crowded together.

If you have walls of a neutral color, foliage and flowering plants of vivid colors will provide sharp accent. However, with colorful background walls, it is wise to stick with green foliage plants.

When shopping for plants, ask the florist for growing recommendations—amount of light, heat, water, and plant food needed for each variety.

Regardless of the section of the country in which you live, there are many plant varieties available that will thrive year-round. So, why not let houseplants perform their green magic in your rooms?

If you want to add a homespun touch to your kitchen, start by using an old roaster like the one above, or another castoff, and use it for a planter. Scrub the roaster well to remove any deposits of grease, and spray-paint it with an aerosol bomb. Fasten two light-weight wire chains to the handles, and suspend it from hooks mounted on the ceiling. For drainage, cover the bottom of the planter with an inch of gravel. Set plants in soil. The cost: about $2.

MAKE USE OF WHAT YOU HAVE

To make the best possible use of houseplants throughout your home, add to their natural beauty by putting them in an attractive planter or container. If you make an exhaustive search in your own home, you will probably find many items that can be used for this purpose.

Even some of the most unlikely items can make interesting habitats for plants. For example, use an oval copper tray to hold two clay pots of caladium plants with their large, heart-shaped leaves. Or load a teacart, one that's easy to wheel from one spot to another, with pots of pink azaleas, pink and white hyacinths, red and white tulips, yellow daffodils, and African violets. This presents a mass of color in a room with neutral tones. If you have room large enough for a plant to spread out its decorative foliage, use one of the 20 varieties of dieffenbachia and set the pot in a wicker basket tall enough to conceal the clay pot. Bowls, pitchers, and compotes of brass, copper, pewter, and earthenware are all likely candidates for displaying greenery.

If you have a flat container of metal, ceramic, or plastic, why not plant a dish garden in it? It can't be too shallow, as most plants need at least three inches of depth for stability and the growth of roots. Select foliage plants with pleasing contrast. Include a variety of height, leaf shape, size, and patterning. Provide drainage with a good bottom layer of pebbles, charcoal, or pieces of broken clay pots.

Even large brandy snifters or old goldfish bowls can be used to house plants. Get a piece of glass to fit the top, and plant a terrarium in it. Once a glass garden has been planted, it needs little water, as the moist air is trapped inside. Use small-scaled plants and place each one so that it is a pleasing contrast of shape and color with its neighbors—variegated foliage next to the solid, colorful next to green, and so on.

Family hand-me-downs are one of the best sources of planters. An old shaving mug, or a pewter mug can hold one or two small plants. Old copper, brass, or iron kitchen utensils—pots, pans, teakettles—are ideal for foliage plants. Earthenware crocks, once used for making and storing pickles, provide a good neutral background for colorful flowering plants. An old coffee grinder, or an obsolete corn sheller can be used as planters for graceful ivy plants.

The dwarf form of crape-myrtle, a southern favorite with crinkled blooms, flowers in delicate clusters in a redwood pot all summer long. When the first cold wave hits, move the plant inside and keep it as cool as you can throughout the winter months.

A classic Florentine lavabo planter with elaborately carved scrolls and acanthus leaves in gold, blue, and green tones against a background of deep red can hold real or artificial greenery. Basin is 23 inches wide, 8¼ inches high, and 7 inches deep; top is 14½ x 20 inches high. It retails for about $50.

BUYING PLANT CONTAINERS

When you shop for a planter or container for houseplants, keep in mind the decor of the room in which the plant will be displayed. Consider the mood of the room—whether it's formal or informal; the style of furnishings—traditional, contemporary, or country; and the background colors. In a room that has a neutral background, you can use foliage plants in containers that are colorful and ornate or flowering plants in simple containers; if the background colors are lively, use foliage plants in containers of subdued colors and simple lines. Also, choose a planter or container that is large enough to allow for healthy plant growth.

Greenery looks especially beautiful in metal containers. There are brass planters in all sizes and shapes—long, narrow ones that can fit on a window sill or an open shelf, hanging planters suspended by chains from wall brackets, and round and oval bowls—in antiqued or shiny

Here, double white petunias contrast with the deep green of the ceramic hanging basket. Besides petunias, consider hanging vining geraniums, alyssum, fountain plants, dwarf marigolds, or succulents in sunny spots. Tuberous begonias, dwarf impatiens, coleus, and sprengeri fern grow better in a shady spot.

finishes. A copper teakettle, tea canister, or cooking pot makes a handsome planter for green foliage plants. A pewter bowl, pitcher, or compote offers a dramatic contrast to either plants with shiny green leaves or velvety leaves.

Items of earthenware or ironstone are available in many designs and sizes. You can use a casserole or soup tureen to hold several different varieties of plants, or a sugar bowl, compote, or creamer to hold a single small plant. If you collect unusual or antique cups and saucers, you could plant an African violet or an ivy plant in each one, and arrange them on a window ledge or on an open shelf.

There are inexpensive wicker and wire baskets, in many shapes and sizes, that can be used as planters. For these, use plants that are growing in clay pots, and simply place one or more of the potted plants in the decorative basket.

In many areas of the country, there is an abundance of handcrafted ceramic bowls, pitchers, and mugs that make ideal planters. You can find these one-of-a-kind items at art centers, and at local art fairs where artists exhibit their wares.

For a contemporary look, choose unadorned planters with simple, straight lines. There are ceramic ones in many colors with either a high-gloss or matte finish; and wood containers with a dull, hand-rubbed finish.

The Celeste fig tree above resembles a rugged little oak tree to those who are not familiar with this variety. The trunk and stems are angular and architectural. A potted fig tree, because of its sturdy constitution, can stay outdoors year-round in mild climates. If the mercury drops to less than 20° above in your area of the country, you can bring the tree inside for the winter months. Even a small fig tree will provide a harvest of fruit for you to enjoy.

The dwarf Bonanza peach tree shown at the left grows well in a large planter. Its only requirement is that it be exposed to direct sunlight. Your dwarf peach tree will go through several distinct changes each year—first, pink fragrant blossoms in the spring of the year; followed by glossy, clustered leaves; and then, bright and colorful, full-sized peaches at midsummer. The dwarf Bonanza is a hardy tree, and can remain outside during the winter months.

PLANTERS YOU CAN BUILD

Planters are inexpensive to build, and do not require expert carpentry skills. Almost anyone who is handy with a hammer and saw can put together a planter that is both decorative and practical.

The chief advantage in building your own plant boxes is that you can modify the dimensions to suit your individual needs. The size you build will depend on the number of plants you want the planter to hold, and how much space the different varieties require for healthy plant growth. Also, a planter should be scaled to the size of the room, or area where it will be used.

If a planter is intended primarily for indoor use, it is a good idea to mount casters on a recessed base at the bottom. This makes it easy

You don't need any tools to build the plant stand below. Use two 15-inch hardwood turnings and a ball finial (buy these at your building supply dealer) for each leg. Get two pieces of ½-inch thick glass, cut in circles 14 inches in diameter. Have ¾-inch holes drilled in one circle to accommodate threaded dowels that connect spindles. Cost: about $25.

To build the planters shown above, cut a piece of exterior plywood one-foot square for the bottom, and cedar 2 x 2s for the two-foot square collar. Connect the corners of both pieces so that the collar is one foot high, and fasten on two horizontal nailing strips. Then, apply inch-thick redwood strips for the flared sides. Work out from the middle of each side and cut as you go for the corners. Staining is optional.

Display your African violet plants on a lazy susan plant stand that revolves to get uniform light. Use ¾-inch plywood for the circular pieces, surfaced with laminated plastic sheeting. Stain the legs to match the laminate and mount to plywood circle fitted under the bottom shelf. It swivels easily on a six-inch lazy susan bearing mounted under the center post. Materials for this plant stand will cost about $19.

A few glazed bricks have been arranged to provide a frame for potted houseplants. You can move philodendron, fern, palm, and schefflera outdoors during the summer months, but start with exposing them to early morning or late afternoon sun, as few houseplants can stand direct sun all day long right at first.

Even in a high rise apartment, you can have your own garden on the balcony. The brackets on the balcony railing hold potted flowers that can be changed with the seasons. A shallow metal box holds a small-scaled sculpture, a variety of pebbles and rocks, and potted plants instead of permanent installations.

to move the plant box from one location to another whenever the plants need a change in temperature and amount of natural sunlight.

If you want a really unique plant stand that will go with any style of furnishings, build a 6-inch high plant display table that gains its inspiration from the Japanese. Cut the tabletop from a sheet of perforated hardboard in a lacy pattern. Form the legs from a 1 x 6-inch board, making gentle, flowing cuts along the bottom of the front and back pieces and around the corners over the legs. Use 2 x 2-inch boards to make the end and bottom braces. Paint the finished table in a pleasing color that contrasts with the various plant colors, and arrange a wide variety of potted plants in an interesting grouping. This type of plant stand is ideal for use in a room with carpeted floors, as the flower pots never touch the carpet.

For an unusual planter with a true designer appearance that will add sparkle to any room, simply stack 10-inch standard and azalea clay,

The planter below is easy to build. Cut plywood to the size you want. Fasten the pieces together to form a box, and attach pressed wood fiber plaques to each side of the planter for detailing. Paint the outside, and seal the inside with fiber glass. To insure proper drainage, place a layer of gravel in the bottom before you fill the planter with soil.

The concrete planter above costs about $7 to build. Use four 3½-inch square concrete blocks and group them around a 16-inch redwood 4 x 4. Drill holes through the wood block, and run wires through them and around the spacers between the holes in the concrete blocks. Plant some green and variegated peperomia and variegated jade plants in the planter.

Even a very small entryway can gain impact from a planter like the one above. The planter is merely a hardwood plywood box with a metal or fiber glass lining. The verticals are finished strips of matching hardwood. Combine both tall and low plants for a dramatic effect. This planter costs about $48.

or ceramic pots one on top of another until you get the height and design you want. Then, glue the pot rims together with epoxy glue. A planter made of three large pots costs about $4.

Glamorizing ordinary clay pots is easy if you make a decorative metal mesh cylinder to slip over the pots. Cut the wire mesh with tin snips, and fasten the ends together by crimping the metal tips of the cut edges through the holes of the adjoining mesh. Spray-paint each cylinder. These cost approximately 75¢ each for materials.

You can make planters and pots from cement colored with special concrete coloring. Get sacks of premixed concrete with lots of aggregate. Add the dry color and less water than is called for. Mix thoroughly, and then press the heavy mixture into plastic pans and buckets to mold into shape. Make a drainage hole in the bottom of each one. When the concrete is dry, flex the plastic containers to release them. You can make several planters and pots for about $6.

Make one 34 x 34-inch and two 17 x 34-inch modular trays to display houseplants, and have tray liners made of galvanized metal. Place each one on a smaller base made with four-inch deep sides and a plywood bottom. Set them on one-inch flat-mount casters. The material for all three will cost about $21.

You can create personal treasures
that you'll cherish and enjoy for years
to come. Handcrafted items beautify the
home in a unique way. Some may even
qualify as collectors' items. Even if
they fail to fall in this classification,
the fact that they are your own
handiwork makes them precious
possessions to you and to your family.

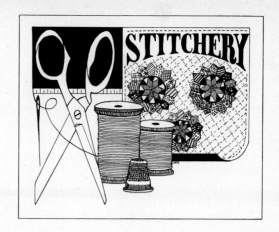

STITCHERY & CRAFTS

You can stretch your decorating funds to the utmost, and have fun at the same time when you make handcrafted items for your home. This is your opportunity to add an individual touch.

Stitchery and craft items are personal treasures that you'll cherish and enjoy for many years to come, and they are well worth the hours of leisure time you spend creating them. Many items can be completed in just one evening; others may require several months to finish, or even longer. It's up to you to decide just how much time to devote to making something unique for your home.

Some handcraft projects can be accomplished by cutting and pasting; others may require special skills. You can develop these skills by enrolling in a class that is taught by a competent instructor. Other skills can be learned by observing family members and friends who are working on stitchery and craft projects. Still others can be mastered by following instructions in books.

If you're one of the lucky ones who is naturally talented and creative, you can tackle the most complicated projects. Even if you're merely a nimble-fingered, but willing beginner, you can start with a simple project. This will give you the confidence necessary to advance to more complex items for your home.

In the stitchery category, there are a lot of techniques: sewing, knitting, hooking rugs, crocheting, appliqueing, weaving, crewel and teneriffe, hand embroidery, and quilting.

In the area of crafts, there are equally as many: collages, felt projects, paper crafts, metal crafts, mosaics, plastics, macramé, stenciling, silk screening, rosemaling, decoupage, woodworking.

As you explore the wide, wide world of stitchery and crafts, you will discover many more techniques besides those mentioned above. Treat each project with loving care. Who knows, the handcrafted item you make today may be a prized heirloom in the years to come.

STITCHERY PROJECTS

A sewing needle can be used for many more interesting jobs than merely stitching seams. Regardless of whether you do your needlework projects with the assistance of a sewing machine or by hand, you can sew a great number of distinctive and useful items for your home, your family, and your friends. Knitting needles, crochet hooks, and looms are also important tools for stitchery projects. Besides the personal satisfaction gained when you make something yourself, there is an additional reward—getting the most value from your decorating dollars.

Unless you are an experienced seamstress, start out with simple designs and patterns—pillows, place mats, wall hangings—until you feel confident that the finished items have a professional look. Then, you can branch out and tackle more complicated projects such as quilted bedspreads, and knitted or crocheted afghans.

Quilting. What once was done painstakingly by hand a stitch at a time is now done almost exclusively on the sewing machine. This means that quilts, throws, and pillow tops can be done in a fraction of the time it once took.

The first step in any quilting project is to determine the amount of fabric you need for the three layers—top, backing, and filler. The fabric for the top can be a solid color, a patterned fabric, or a patchwork design made by machine-stitching pieces of different colors and patterns in whatever design you choose. You will need fabric of a harmonizing color for the backing, and the same amount of filler—either cotton flannel, or cotton or Dacron batting.

Next, plan the quilting design. If you use a solid color for the top, trace or draw your quilting design on the fabric. If you use a patterned fabric, quilt around the patterns for the quilting design. If the top has a patchwork design, stitch about ⅛ inch inside all of the seams. Baste all

You can keep cherished records of baby forever with this sampler wall hanging. It can be made in just a few relaxing hours. This kit includes the design stamped on linen, embroidery thread, 11x14-inch frame, carbon paper, and instructions. (To obtain kit, order No. 00481 from Reader Service, 9AN, 1716 Locust St., Des Moines, Iowa 50336.)

You can stitch this 'Serenity Prayer' wall hanging. It's easy to do—a simple cross-stitch—and very economical. Kit includes design stamped on fine quality linen, embroidery floss, and complete instructions. Sampler fits inside 14x18-inch hardwood frame. (To obtain kit, order No. 00302 from Reader Service, 9AN, 1716 Locust St., Des Moines, Iowa 50336.)

three layers together—the top, filler, and backing—beginning in the center and working outward to the edges of the fabric.

Now, you are ready to start quilting. Use either a machine quilting attachment on your sewing machine, or quilt by hand. If you are quilting by hand, fasten the three layers to a quilt frame. Regardless of whether you are quilting by machine or by hand, start in the center of the piece and work outward in all directions.

After the entire piece is quilted, run a careful, straight line of machine stitching around the edges, and trim the edges evenly.

Whether you're making a large quilt top or a small pillow top, the same instructions apply to all quilting projects you undertake.

Knitting. The abundance of yarn in an exciting array of colors, textures, and materials available today makes knitting for the home a popular pastime. You can knit afghans, wall hangings, place mats, and covers for pillows and chair cushions. The only supplies that you need are a variety of knitting yarns—wool, synthetic, cotton, or a blend; mohair, straw, or metallic—and knitting needles. Couple these with some knowledge of the basic stitches, and knitting will become an interesting hobby.

You can knit a colorful afghan of either four-ply knitting worsted, or of cloud-soft mohair yarn. Select a pattern and colors that accent your room's decor, and make it large enough to be used as a throw—at least 48 x 65 inches.

Brighten up a dining area with colorful hand-knit chair cushions and place mats. Cut the chair cushions from ⅝-inch thick foam rubber to fit the chair seats, and knit the covers of knitting worsted. Combine several colors of yarn in the design, and add matching ties to hold them securely to the chair seats. Make the place mats of linen yarn, choosing a color that is identical to one of those that appears in the cushions.

It's easy to freshen older throw pillows whose covers have grown drab and faded. Just knit covers for them of standard knitting worsted. Use lively colors of yarn, and simple knitting stitches. This is a quick and effective way to give any room a lift with very little expense.

A handsome wall hanging can be knitted from synthetic straw (shiny raffia) yarn. This knits up very rapidly on large needles. Make it to measure 21 x 76 inches. Attach it to a wood frame, and mount it to the wall at ceiling height.

You can make this washable green wool table cover with a textured wool applique for about $8. The large plant forms of the design divide the cloth into four settings. You can extend the same design for more seating. The applique runs to the edges of the tablecloth, thus showing the design from all sides of the table. Cut some extra shapes from the wool that was used on the cloth and applique them to sets of solid color linen napkins that you can buy ready-made.

A group of pillows—with machine-sewed applique designs—like those pictured below add sharp color contrast to any room. Use a satin-stitch or solid zig-zag-stitch at full width on large pieces; narrower width on smaller pieces. Use scraps of fabric for the designs, or cut the shapes from felt. Pin each piece in place carefully before you start to sew them on. You can make an assortment of pillows in different sizes and shapes for about $5.

Chair Seat Cover   **Pansy Pillow**   **Jacobean Pillow**

This exclusive design for chair seat covers is adapted from American Indian art. Only three basic crewel embroidery stitches are needed to create this design. Kit comes complete with stamped design on a 28x28-inch piece of imported linen, crewel yarns, needle, and easy-to-follow instructions. Order kit No. 00440. For a matching 14x14-inch pillow, order kit No. 00441.

The pansy pillow, with its bright colors, is a round 14x2-inch box pillow that will bring springtime freshness to any room. Kit comes complete with design stamped on lime linen for entire pillow, 2-inch-wide boxing strip, matching piping, brilliant crewel embroidery yarns in gold, orange, and purple, zipper, needle, and instructions. Order kit No. 00453.

Colorful crewel stitchery in a graceful Jacobean design adorns this 14-inch-square knife-edge pillow. Kit includes stamped linen, cording, zipper, wool embroidery yarn, and instructions. Order kit No. 00458. (To obtain kits, order from Reader Service, 9AN, 1716 Locust St., Des Moines, Iowa 50336.)

Appliqueing. Appliqueing is simply the method of sewing a motif cut from fabric on top of another piece of fabric. This is a golden opportunity to give ordinary look-alike items that one-of-a-kind custom appearance. With a minimum of time and effort you can applique lovely designs on either handmade or ready-made household items. Bedspreads, sheets, pillow cases, headboards, towels, table linens, pillows, chair covers, wall hangings, and fabric-covered patio furniture are all ideal candidates for applique trim. It can be done by hand or machine.

When appliqueing by hand, trace your design on the applique fabric and cut it out, allowing ¼-inch seam allowance. Machine stitch just outside the tracing line, then turn under the seam allowance just inside the machine stitch-ing. Pin the design in place on the item you are decorating, and sew around the design with either a slip-stitch or a blanket-stitch.

For machine applique, cut out the applique design, allowing ¼-inch seam allowance. Stitch the design in place by machine, using a fine zigzag-stitch. Then, trim away the excess material around the stitching, and restitch around the edge, using a satin-stitch set full width.

Use applique designs to add a playful accent to a small child's bedroom. Cut out bird, duck, or bunny motifs and applique them on the borders of contrasting color sheets, pillow cases, and towels, using machine stitching. You can also add originality to an inexpensive, ready-made quilted bedspread by appliqueing larger versions of the same motifs around lower edge.

Crocheting. A fine, old art that added grace and beauty to the homes of the early settlers of our country has recently taken on a new look to complement modern-day furnishings. The easy-to-learn basic stitches remain just the same, but there's a fresh approach—using them to add textural accent to simple fabrics.

First, crochet yards and yards of chains, braids, and fringes. Use different weights and textures of yarn; combine several strands of yarn in closely related, vibrant shades. Then, apply these trims to fabric with glue, creating your own designs as you go. The type of adhesive you use is determined by whether the fabric is one that must be laundered or dry cleaned.

Use crocheted motifs in graduated sizes to decorate a fabric room divider. Dress up place mats, draperies, or a tablecloth with a sophisticated scroll border, created by crocheting a simple fringe from soft, bulky yarn. Trim several plain-color pillows with designs that combine several crochet stitches, or use a simple chain.

In this coordinated bolster and window treatment, the designs are worked with gift-tie yarn and then stitched down with embroidery floss. First, place the fabric on pieces of wax paper to keep it from sticking to your work surface. Practice drawing on paper, then draw on fabric with a soft lead pencil. Go over penciled pattern with white glue. Lay gift-tie yarn on glued outline and let dry thoroughly so it will not slip from its position. Complete gluing of all areas, then stitch across with floss at ¼-inch intervals from inside to out. Vary look with different sized stitches or different colors of embroidery floss.

The snail designs are easy-to-draw spirals. To achieve different effects, place spirals closer together, or farther apart. Besides the regulation couching stitch, you can achieve dramatic effects with a cross-stitch or a buttonhole-stitch. Use extra stitches on corners, curves, and points.

To tie-dye a tablecloth like the one above, use a yellow linen tablecloth and fold it in half lengthwise. Tie securely, and dye the cloth with a brown color. Retie it at other points and dye dark brown. Retie cloth and immerse in dye color remover. Rinse, then immerse it in a gray dye.

CRAFT PROJECTS

Some craft projects are so simple that the youngest members of the family can master them. Others require patience, time, and special skills to produce something that is truly creative. Between these two extremes there is a long list of craft techniques, many of which are appropriate for making decorative and useful items.

Hobby shops and art supply dealers carry a wide variety of craft materials, and new and even more exciting ones keep cropping up. For example, there are plastic materials, brilliant papers and paints, protective sprays, adhesives for every use, and an assortment of handy tools.

There are many items that can be made of felt, mosaics, and papier mâché. However, if you're the "string saver" type, you probably have a supply of ordinary materials that will provide the makings for many craft projects. String, coffee cans, paper bags, plastic berry baskets, scraps of fabric and felt, and the hollow cardboard tubes from rolls of food wrap are just a few of the castaways that you can use. Paper cups, pasta, coat hangers, and aluminum foil are other supplies that can be transformed into unusual objects.

Felt. This popular choice for craft projects is easy to work with, inexpensive, comes in widths of up to 72 inches, and is available in a wide range of vivid colors. Because it is non-woven material, it doesn't ravel, and it isn't necessary to finish the edges. However, not all felt is of the same quality. Felt may be all wool, part wool, or cotton. All wool is the most expensive; cotton, the least expensive. You can use the less expensive varieties for items such as wall hangings, table runners, holiday decorations, or anything that receives little wear. When it comes to pillows, rugs, and chair covers, buy a good quality of felt.

Bright pillows made of felt are a welcome addition to any room. Cut the felt to size to fit the pillows you are covering, allowing excess for a seam allowance. Cut out felt motifs of colors that are harmonious with the background color, and stitch the applique designs in place. Choose designs that suit the mood of your furnishings. They can be floral, abstract, or geometric—arranged on the pillow top in whatever pattern pleases you. Combine several shapes of pillows—square, triangular, rectangular, or round—in a grouping. Spray them with a fabric finisher so that they will resist soil.

Make a wall hanging with brightly colored flowers cut out of felt and mounted on a panel of hardboard covered with felt or burlap. Or make a circular tablecloth of felt, add one or

Tie-dyeing is a quick and easy way to revitalize old fabrics or individualize new ones. The step-by-step photos below illustrate how the draperies at the right were dyed. Fold clean, pressed fabric lengthwise in even, two-inch folds. For a sharp crease, iron folds before tying. Tie and knot fabric very tightly at regular intervals. This will help achieve the "plaid" effect. If fabric is not tied tightly, the dye will seep away the design. Do not use porous or colored twine unless you want it to "leak" dye onto fabric. Rubber bands can replace twine if the item is small.

If possible, run a test on fabric before dyeing. This will show how well the dye takes to the fabric. Then, put on rubber gloves and add dye to water in kettle as instructed on dye bottle. As water simmers, immerse tied fabric in mixture from 5 to 15 minutes; then remove. Rinse fabric in cool water until water runs clear. Cut the twine as fabric rinses, being careful not to snip fabric. Should you want to add a second color, wait until the fabric dries, then repeat the process, but tie in different places. When dyeing two or more colors, dye lightest color first.

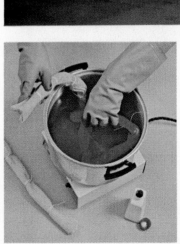

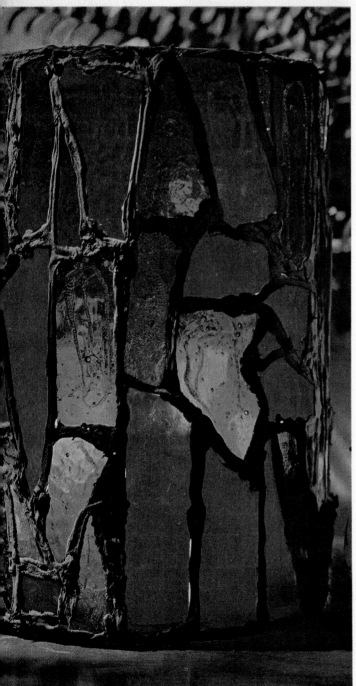

All it takes to make this glistening candle lamp are scraps of stained glass, glue, liquid steel, and a container to cover. When selecting containers to cover with stained glass, remember that straight-sided cylindrical shapes are easier to work with—so choose any tumbler, apothecary jar, or hurricane lamp with straight sides. You can buy glass scraps from a stained glass dealer, or you can make your own by applying stained glass paint to plain window glass.

First, place the glass pieces in a small cardboard box, covering them with brown paper. Now, use a hammer to break the glass into bits. Apply stained glass to the container with a glass glue or clear transparent glue. Gauge the size of the pieces so they'll be in scale with the container. Vary the colors of glass as you apply the bits, leaving a small space between each one. As the glue dries, slowly rotate the container. Squeeze the tube of liquid steel between the pieces of stained glass. Build to the desired thickness. It will dry in solid metal strips.

more rows of braid or fringe around the bottom. Add a feminine touch to a mirror with a plain frame by covering the frame with flowers cut out of felt. For the Christmas holidays, make table runners, place mats, felt wreaths, door decorations, and Christmas stockings of felt. Trim these items with ribbon, braid, yarn, and sequins.

Mosaic. Basically, this art is the same as it was centuries ago. Small pieces of stone, tile, stained glass, or metal are anchored with glue and grout to form decorative designs. Today, mosaic projects for the home include ash trays, trivets, trays, tabletops, and wall murals.

In addition to the tile, you will need a cutter, glue, and grout. You can find these items in a hardware store or hobby shop. Unfinished plywood makes a sturdy frame for a large mosaic piece—a wall mural or tabletop. If you want a transparent effect, use framed, double-strength glass for the backing. When you are making small items, glue the tiles on tin cans, or bases that you can purchase at a hobby shop.

Whatever your project—tabletop, ash tray, wall mural—first, cut a piece of heavy paper to the exact size and shape. Then, arrange the pieces of tile, glass, stone, or metal on the paper in the design you want. Spread the adhesive in small amounts on the plywood, metal, or glass backing you are using, and transfer the tiles, one at a time, from the paper to the backing, sticking them firmly into the glue. After you have completed the design, fill in the space between the tiles with grouting of cement mixed with water to a creamy consistency. With a gloved hand, spread the grout over the dry tiles, pressing it firmly into the crevices. After about five minutes, wipe off the excess grout. Then, let the project stand for about ten hours to dry. Wash it thoroughly to remove any residue of grout, and to clean the pieces of tile.

Even if you're all thumbs and none of them is green, you can "grow" these flamboyant yarn flowers. You will need an assortment of different colored yarns, wire, florist's tape, spray adhesive, cardboard, scissors, and a hairbrush. Cut three sizes of cardboard, 6 x 3-inches, 4 x 3-inches, and 2 x 3-inches. Wrap each rectangle with a different color yarn. Cut the yarn at both ends, and tie tightly in the center. Spread out the yarn in a circle. With a regular hairbrush, brush in short strokes away from the center. Spray the back of each medium-sized flower with white glue, and press onto a large one. Repeat with the pompons. Use coat hangers or wire to make the stems. Cover the wires with green florist's tape, and attach them to the backs of the flowers with a loop of yarn. For the leaves, wrap the yarn around a six-inch cardboard. Cut one end, and tie the other. Brush them, and trim to shape. To clean, dust them with a hairbrush.

The basic forms for these trays are pulp paper liners used to contain fruits and meats in the supermarket. Be sure to obtain two of each size as you will glue two together for each section, making a more rigid form. Other materials you will need include dry, ground gesso which dries to a hard, plasterlike finish. Follow directions for mixing, then apply three coats of gesso to trays that have been glued together. When gesso is dry, the tray becomes rigid and is ready to be smoothed with sandpaper. Spray-paint with flat black enamel, and edge with gilt. Decorate the base with gold and turquoise mosaic pattern paper (it is adhesive-backed plastic).

Papier mâché. Ordinary newspapers take on a regal role, as did Cinderella when the Prince fitted the glass slipper on her foot, when they are part of papier mâché. It's a little- or no-cost craft that you can use to create captivating items for the home—candlesticks, sculptured objects, holiday decorations, whimsical animals for children. Even the novice can accomplish amazing results with little instruction.

Old newspapers, flour, and water or a new commercial mixture available at hobby shops, are the basic materials you need. Then, add an assortment of containers, wire coat hangers, balloons, and Styrofoam shapes to provide bases.

Tear the newspaper into narrow strips, several thicknesses at a time—always tearing it rather than cutting it to avoid blunt edges. Coat the base with a layer of paste, using a two-inch paint brush, and cover the base with strips of newspaper. Continue alternating layers of paste and newspaper until you have built up the base into the desired form. Apply only a few layers at one time. When the paste is thoroughly dry, paint the object with acrylic or poster paint.

You can make towering candlesticks that glow with gemlike Byzantine luster with the papier mâché method. First, arrange a series of discards such as jars, lids, cans, plastic containers, and bowls one on top of another to gain the desired height, experimenting with several arrangements to see which has the most pleasing proportions. Then, glue them together. At the very top, use an inverted container to hold the candle.

Next, cover the surface with a layer of papier mâché, using narrow strips and small squares of newspaper. Brush one small area with glue, then apply the paper; then brush on more glue and apply more paper, overlapping the edges slightly. When the entire surface has been covered, apply a coat of gesso and allow it to dry.

The next step is to add the trim, and this is your opportunity to be as inventive as you want.

Use cord or twine, shell or elbow macaroni, lace, or braid. Glue these on the candlestick whereever you want to add motifs or borders. After you have applied all the trim, use glue again to brush over the trim and allow to dry.

Now, you are ready to paint. If you use the dry-brush method, apply an undercoat of black acrylic paint to cover the surface. When this is dry, dry-brush it with a little paint on the brush in a contrasting shade. Drag the brush across the surface of the candleholder only, allowing the textures and recesses to show through. Or you can use the rub method of antiquing. Paint various design areas with different colors of artist's paint. Let the paint dry, then cover the entire surface with raw umber. Work it into the small areas. When it is just dry, rub it off with a clean cloth, leaving some of the dark color in the recesses and around the trim. Finish with one or two coats of clear glaze.

Here's a potpourri of colorful decorative ideas from which to choose. These are all easy-to-make, practical items decorated with felt tip markers. Test the pen on a sample of the fabric before you start the actual decorating; if the ink runs, stretch the fabric. Sketch your designs on paper first, then trace the pattern with a pencil onto the felt, fabric, or plastic material that you are decorating. Use felt tip pens to follow designs.

You can use awning-striped paper cups to hold bouquets of violets, cornflowers, and daisies. These do-it-yourself flower containers can be made in minutes. Simply glue hot drink cups together. To achieve different heights, vary the number of cups in a stack. Group several containers together, add a pair of candlesticks and candles, and you will have a striking centerpiece for an informal occasion.

Use laundry room treasures to create the casual centerpiece containers above. The bowl is made by slicing the top from a gallon plastic bottle, then trimming the cut edge into points, and rolling the points outward with a pencil. The jug is simply a gallon jug in its original form. Paint both of them to complement the colors of your flowers, and trim them with rows of raffia glued tightly together.

CENTERPIECES

Craft decorations and accessories help to establish a festive mood. Whether you're planning a formal sit-down dinner, a breakfast on the patio, or a buffet supper, a lovely centerpiece is an indication that the hostess has taken particular care in all her preparations. A table set with special attention makes dining with family and friends a very important event.

Follow the same rules that apply to all other areas of interior design. It's a combination of color, scale, and proportion, along with attractive colors that give the centerpiece eye appeal. Also, the table, the centerpiece, and the large and small objects on the table should all be scaled to the size of the dining area. Be sure that they are in proportion to each other, too. For example, if you're using candles, their height should be compatible with the height of the centerpiece and your crystal stemware.

Many times you want to keep the centerpiece low, and small-scaled. Here's one suggestion on how to do this. Use a cream pitcher and a sugar bowl as containers—either glass, porcelain, or earthenware. Place the pitcher on a stand so that the two pieces will be of different heights. Arrange a quantity of tiny mums, correctly scaled to the size of the containers. Mass the flowers at the base of the containers for a low line, and place the tall stems at an angle. This particular type of centerpiece will present a quaint and charming effect, suitable for many occasions.

On another occasion, you may prefer a tall and stately centerpiece with a contemporary feeling. You can achieve this mood by stacking long-stemmed glasses to form three towers of different heights. Fit the goblets base-to-base, and elevate some of them on stands or small dishes to create an unusual silhouette. If you don't have glasses of the right hue, you can spray-paint them in colors to match your flowers, or to contrast with them. Place a small, casual bouquet of bright pink roses in each skyscraper, and stand back to admire your handiwork.

If your cupboard shelters the remnants of sets of broken glassware, use these stray pieces to serve as containers for an unusual floral centerpiece. Combine several glass bowls of different sizes and shapes with one tall tumbler, and group them on a small oval tray. Place clusters of vivid carnations in each container, and add a dramatic touch with large, smooth-textured leaves fixed at right angles to the flower clusters.

You don't always need live flowers to create a beautiful centerpiece. It's easy to make a colorful centerpiece of pseudo-sunflowers. Cut the flowers from paper place mats, and glue them back-to-back to green pipe cleaner stems. Cut several circles of the same material, and roll

them to simulate buds. Make the leaves of four thicknesses of leaf green paper napkins. Arrange the flowers casually in a berry box.

Use candles anytime to change an ordinary meal into a festive banquet. You can create an Egyptian atmosphere by using several distinctive, sculptured candles in a unique centerpiece. Take two ordinary building bricks (with ready-made holes through them) and spray-paint them black and use as candleholders. Complete the Nile scene with an inexpensive plaster statue, and straw place mats sprayed black.

Only a few of the many craft techniques have been touched upon in this chapter. Whether you're a beginner or an experienced craftsman, your skills will improve with each project you undertake. If you want detailed help in any specific craft, consult libraries and bookshops.

The elements used in this centerpiece for a "Last Night to Crow" (New Year's Eve) party take on a new look. A red burlap tablecloth is bordered with ball fringe. An inverted wicker basket is used as a stand for a rooster candle cover of wrought iron. An arrangement of magnolia leaves, milo corn heads, Italian wheat, and candles add the finishing touches.

If you have wood paneling in rich, dark colors, you can create a centerpiece with an authentic medieval mood. Use several sizes and colors of roughly textured candles that provide just enough light for a pleasant dining atmosphere. Use pewter serving pieces if you have them. Otherwise, use dark-colored pottery for an equally effective "Old World" theme.

INDEX

160

ACKNOWLEDGEMENTS FOR PHOTOGRAPHS

Arabesque, a division of Burwood
    Products Company

Armstrong Cork Company

Arno Adhesive Tapes, Inc.

Bigelow-Sanford Carpet Company

Colorific House

Galway, a division of Burwood

Mutschler Kitchens

Rug Corporation of America

Russ Stonier, Inc.

Tyndale, Inc.

Window Shade Manufacturers Assoc.